BUDDHISM
FOR THE
WEST

❀ THERAVĀDA

❀ MAHĀYĀNA

❀ VAJRAYĀNA

BUDDHISM
FOR THE WEST

* THERAVĀDA

* MAHĀYĀNA

and

* VAJRAYĀNA

A comprehensive review of Buddhist history, philosophy, and teachings from the time of the Buddha to the present day

DOROTHY C. DONATH

McGraw-Hill Book Company

New York · St. Louis · San Francisco · Düsseldorf
Mexico · Montreal · Panama · São Paulo · Toronto

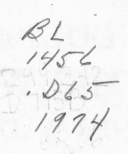
Buddhism for the West

Library of Congress Catalog Card Number: 78-170948
Book design by Ernst Reichl Associates

Reprinted by arrangement with The Julian Press, Inc.

First McGraw-Hill Paperback Edition, 1974

0-07-017533-0

1 2 3 4 5 6 7 8 9 MU MU 7 9 8 7 6 5 4

CONTENTS

Blessings in the Dharma
To all sentient beings

FOREWORD

Why I became a Buddhist is one of the questions I am most often asked. Here is my answer:

I became a Buddhist because Buddhism (the Buddha-Dharma) is a religion of reason: it is pragmatic but at the same time preeminently of the Spirit—and so a deeply satisfying way of life; because it imposes no creeds or dogmas and demands no submission to or blind faith in any separate deity, person, or thing, and thus is devoid of every dualistic belief and concept; because it teaches unity with all life everywhere, and compassion for every living being, man and animal alike; because it accords to man the beauty and dignity of original perfection, not original sin, and shows him the way by means of his own efforts, intuitive insights, and growing realization to uncover this perfection—his real and intrinsic Buddha-nature—which is Enlightenment itself; and finally, I became a Buddhist because Buddhism affirms that the Cosmos, with all its evolving worlds in all their relative reality, is not a "creation" in specific time by any personal God or Being, however transcendent, but is a manifestation, an outpouring, of universal Infinite Intelligence, Mind—the only *Ultimate* Reality, of which every sentient being is a part and in which all life everywhere shares—never static, but forever folding and unfolding in the Way of Ultimate Truth, without beginning and without end.

I hope the following pages will help to demonstrate for my readers, at least in part, the priceless truths I have been privileged to learn.[1]

INTRODUCTION

The following chapters represent a journey of dis-
covery in Buddhism over the past twelve years. That
journey's beginnings, in time, were long ago; its end
is not yet and may never be, for "a beginning" and
"an end" exist only in the realm of relative thought.
But these few steps, historical and spiritual, which
may, hopefully, be of help to others on the same
road, are here set down as they have revealed themselves to me.

The chapters are not arranged in the chrono-
logical order in which they, or the sections within
them, were originally written, but in a sequence
which has nothing to do with time. They are presented, insofar as I am able, in an order of growth,
mental and spiritual, which cannot fall into any
logical set pattern such as might be represented on a
graph, in the framework of time and space. Intuition transcends time; and space, real on one level, is

a mental construct on another. If the material herein assembled serves as one pointer to that Reality to be found in all life and in the inner being of every man, it has served its purpose well. "A finger pointing to the moon," as we have been told many times, is not the moon itself—although it may suggest a way thereto; but to walk on the moon, and to venture into the infinite Universe beyond is a divine and human prerogative which each adventurer, in unity with Nature and with that Cosmic Principle which some call God, must discover and take for himself.

Chapter 1, "The Buddha and Basic Buddhism—Theravāda and Mahāyāna," is a detailed resumé of Buddhism's basic teachings, and was first composed in the form of a lecture and delivered to university and college students and to church and lay organizations devoted to a study of comparative religion, or to a special interest in Buddhism—not only as a great religio-philosophic way of life which for more than 2500 years has had an unparalleled influence upon the lives, cultures, and arts of Asia, but one which has now begun to exert an ever-growing impact on the thinking and mores of the West. An earlier version of this chapter, in article form, appeared in a special, May-June, 1966, issue honoring *Vaisākha* (the Buddha's birthday), of *The Maha Bodhi Journal,* Calcutta, India.

The three sections making up Chapter 2 (earlier versions of which were published in *The Maha Bodhi Journal,* in *The Mountain Path,* Tiruvannamalai, Madras, and in *World Buddhism,* Ceylon) trace the development of the Mahāyāna Branch of Buddhism from its earliest beginnings, through the resolution of conflicting ideas as to the nature of Reality proposed by Nāgārjuna in the 2nd century A.D., to the present time, and discuss the subjects of "Destiny" and Reincarnation.

Thus in these two opening chapters I have tried to cover at least a comprehensive introduction to a subject of profound significance, and of growing impact everywhere.

Chapter 3 covers an outline of the special Tibetan form of Buddhism, the Vajrayāna or Diamond Vehicle, arising from the Mahāyāna and other, Tantric, influences in the 8th century; and a résumé of the life and teachings of Milarepa, Tibet's great Poet-Saint—founder, with his famous Guru, Marpa, of the Kargyudpa School of the Tibetan Vajrayāna, and one of its greatest exponents. This chapter, now enlarged and revised, is based upon a lecture given by the author before The Friends of Buddhism of Washington, D.C., in 1964.

(Two shorter articles, "Some Aspects of Buddhist Yoga . . ." and "Milarepa, Tibet's Great Poet-Saint," based on portions of the material in this Chapter, appeared in *The Mountain Path* for July, 1967 and April, 1968, respectively. A third article, "The Kargyudpa School of Tibetan Buddhism," also based on a section of this Chapter, appeared in *The Maha Bodhi Journal*, May-June, 1967.)

Lastly, the two parts of Chapter 4—"In Retrospect: A Dharma Journey" and "From the Well of Meditation," a poem in the Zen spirit—grew from the author's own experiences, and appeared (the first in an earlier, now slightly revised form) in *The Middle Way*, Journal of the Buddhist Society, London; and the second in *The Golden Light*, Penang, and *The Mountain Path*. This Chapter, in the nature of a colophon, creates a kind of personal "signature"— both intuitive and derivative, but above all experiential—arising from depths of the human psyche not "personal" at all.

I am deeply grateful to the teachers and the sources which have made this book possible. May it lead to other beginnings and farther journeys than mine for those who pause to read and ponder. "That he who runs may read" is an aphorism; "That he who pauses to reflect resumes his journey with renewed strength" is equally valid, and perhaps the better way. I leave this to the judgment and understanding of the reader, with blessings in the Dharma to all sentient beings ascending a path to THAT which, in reality, is already with us here and now.

DOROTHY C. DONATH

Washington, D.C.
May 1971

1

THE BUDDHA
AND BASIC BUDDHISM—
THERAVĀDA & MAHĀYĀNA²

INTRODUCTION

As I start to write this chapter the month of May is approaching, and with the first full moon of that month will come *Vaisākha*, the day of the Buddha's birth. No time would be more propitious than this to begin an account of the Buddhist Teaching, and of that great Founder and Teacher, the man Gautama who, more than 2500 years ago, gave to the world a philosophy and Way of Life which has endured and influenced for generations the lives of millions upon millions of people. It is a time, also, in which to remind ourselves that Buddhism (the Buddha-Dharma, or the Buddha-Law as it is called in the East) is a *universal* teaching, and contains a message of inestimable value for all the world in

1

these modern days of strife and turmoil. It can form an indissoluble bond between all peoples if they will but heed its message.

In writing "The Buddha and Basic Buddhism" I have attempted to present here a study of Buddhism as a fundamental *unit*, a *whole*—without bias or distinction as to form, or School, or sect. (Over the centuries many Schools and methods of practice, emphasizing one or another of the Sūtras (Scriptures) or different aspects of the Teachings, have arisen, developed, faded, and arisen again or been replaced by others, according to the times, places, cultural environments, and peoples among whom Buddhism has spread. As earthly time is reckoned, the forms that have proved of value have endured— not as ends in themselves, but as *means* by which men of differing tendencies, times, and levels of understanding have striven to carry forward their spiritual evolution toward Ultimate Enlightenment. All these forms have their value and their place when understood in this light, and not severally or individually *clung to* as the *only* Path. Underlying them all is the *Spirit*, the *Essence* of Buddhism—revealed to us by Gautama from his ineffable experience of Enlightenment; and this, while embracing *all* name and form, transcends them and so eternally remains.

2

Herein lies the basic unity of Buddhism, wherever it may be found.

Buddhism in the West, as elsewhere, is in a process of evolution—the growth and development that all great systems must undergo if they are not to perish. The same forces of adaptation are at work today which have operated with equal vigor in the past—a testament to the strength and underlying vitality of a great religion and way of life that cannot be bound within the narrow limits of any human institution, but preserves its inner integrity no matter in what formal "dress" it may appear. To know past and present forms is good; to dwell upon the underlying Essence of the Buddha-Truth is better; to find one's own Path within that Essence is best of all.

It is these essentials that matter and are needed now—not only in the West but everywhere—as the world struggles in the chaos of transition toward a new birth. It is in this spirit, therefore, that I set down the following thoughts.

FUNDAMENTALS

Let us consider first a form that is almost universal in both East *and* West—the folding of the hands, palm to palm, in reverent greeting or in communion with *That* which each man in his own heart senses as both immanent and transcendent Truth. The discerning Buddhist, in so doing, sees beyond *appearances* and addresses himself with reverence and humility to the true Buddha-nature—the transcendent Spirit both within and without—of which every sentient being, including himself, is a manifestation and a part.

But this is not the only meaning; there are others. The joined hands may signify a simple greeting of friendship and peace or, with a low bow or obeisance, a gesture of special respect or adoration. The higher the hands are raised and the lower the bow, the greater the respect and reverence expressed.

Most importantly, however, and of prime significance, the gesture of joining the two hands symbolizes the coexistence of two inseparable worlds —two aspects of *one* Cosmic life—the material and the spiritual, the static and the dynamic, the world of form and the world of Spirit, or Mind. The right hand symbolizes the realm of Spirit; the left, the realm of beings—the material universe. Other correlatives in this context are positive and negative, active and passive, male and female, noumenon and phenomenon—and there are many more. Union of

4

these "opposites" as symbolized in the joining of two hands, represents the fundamental unity of all things in the *Dharmadhātu*—the universal World of Truth, the Totality of the Infinite Universe—for here, as taught in Buddhism, there is no duality—no "separateness" of the knower from the known, of the individual from his Source.

In Buddhist devotion, when the hands so folded are raised to forehead, lips, and heart, they symbolize the dedication of body, speech, and mind (and in the wider sense, of all form, mantric sound, and thought) to the One Infinite Reality.

Lastly, this gesture is significant not only of the Buddhist, but of the whole Oriental way of thinking—expressed concisely in the three words: "Thesis, antithesis, synthesis." The Westerner *analyzes*—taking every thing and every concept apart to see "how it ticks"; the Easterner *synthesizes*—finding unity in diversity, wholeness in separateness, seeing the *oneness* at the heart of all things, understanding—or sensing intuitively—the One Spirit, Ground of Being, or Buddha-Essence embracing and permeating all.

Thus we see represented in this simple, universal gesture—used in both East *and* West, and characteristic of even the humblest peasant—the two sides of one coin, the two complementary and, if so under-

5

stood, neither antagonistic nor irreconcilable approaches to the same underlying Truth which governs and sustains us all.

Buddhism can be, at the same time, both deep and simple—not only as a religion (in the broadest sense of this term) and a philosophy, but as a whole way of life. It is deep in that it can be a life-long study and practice for the dedicated Buddhist, or the study and endeavor of *many* lifetimes—for to the Buddhist this present life, for most of us, is only a brief stopover (one of many "grades" in the "school" from which we will all ultimately graduate)—a brief stopover for learning and experience in the long journey of life, death, rebirth (either here or elsewhere), and spiritual evolution. I must add that this rebirth, according to Buddhism, is not of the personal ego-soul, which is transient and perishable and upon which we place far too much value, but of our stream of consciousness, or life-force—our *character* —molded by *Karma*, the Law of Cause and Effect— the action and reaction for good or ill, recognized by Christianity in the saying: "As a man soweth so shall he reap," that dominates our lives until Enlightenment—the overcoming of spiritual ignorance and the realization of Ultimate Truth—frees us from it. Thus Buddhism can be a profound study and dedicated practice, with inner meanings and depths of experience undreamed of by the beginner or the uninitiated.

But Buddhism is also simple, in that it teaches the basic ethical practices, in daily living, of unselfishness, compassion, and good-will toward all beings, both human *and* animal. It emphasizes the transiency of all material things; the illusory, impermanent, and unreal nature of the personal ego, or self; and the unity and kinship of all life.

However one embarks upon it, the Buddhist Way is not easy—involving unrelenting practice of self-discipline; of *mindfulness* in all things; of *meditation*, or contemplation to awaken the intuitive mind; and of deep compassion for all living creatures—not as entities separate from ourselves, but as part of our own being, as we are of theirs. Without this living practice, all the intellectual knowledge *about* Buddhism (books, lectures, scriptures, and the like, upon which so much emphasis is placed by most of us) will be of little value.

Buddhism is not based on blind faith in anything written in a book—however "holy"—or preached by any teacher, even the Buddha himself, but on *understanding* (the first step in the Noble Eight-fold Path to be discussed later), gained for oneself through reasoning, study, earnest devotion, meditation, and the practice of the basic ethical principles of selflessness and love. A Buddhist takes no vow of obedience and is offered no rewards or punishments external to himself. Neither "good" nor "evil," nor the concept of "sin" as the West understands it, is preached in Buddhism; but much is said of knowledge *versus* ignorance, that is, of spiritual awareness, wisdom, *versus* the lack of it. He who is wise, says the Buddhist, knows that we are not punished *for* our sins, but *by* them. One is given the knowledge that nothing exists except the idea, the perception, the *mind* through which it is seen or acted upon—for all *is* MIND.

Western science has come very close to this concept when it tells us that *energy*—only a step from pure Consciousness—is at the root and origin of all things. A table, for instance, which appears so solid and so real to our limited physical senses in reality is, as we now know, nothing but a mass of concentrated energy—whirling atoms and electrons, with spaces between them equivalent, on their infinitesimal scale, to the voidnesses, on the cosmic scale, between the planets and the stars. The Buddha knew this, in principle if not in fact, more than 2500 years ago—

long before science as we know it today was even thought of.

Buddhism encourages freedom of thought and a wide tolerance, amazing to some people, as it respects *all* religions as valid expressions, in varying forms suitable to different kinds of people, of the highest understandings and spiritual aspirations of man at different stages on his long evolutionary journey. The true Buddhist never says, "I am right and you are wrong." He believes that while the divine message is *given* differently according to the "wavelengths" of different peoples and times, Ultimate Truth is *One*. The essential unity of Wisdom and Compassion, as symbolized in the iconography, that is, in the images, paintings, and other religious art—particularly in the Northern, or Mahāyāna Branch—is also a fundamental tenet.

Buddhists do *not* worship idols or "graven images." The images to be seen in the temples or on the home shrines of the people are *reminders only* of Gautama, the Buddha, who gave us the Teachings; or of the Bodhisattvas (see pp. 16-18)—representations in personified form of divine qualities or aspects such as Wisdom, Compassion, Spiritual Strength, and the like—to be discussed later in connection with the

9

specific doctrines of the Mahāyāna and the Vajra-yāna. "Rūpa" means form, and the Buddha-rūpa, or Buddha image provides us with a focus of concentration in meditation, and reminds us of the spiritual qualities we seek to awaken in ourselves.

The word "Buddha" (derived from the Sanskrit word *budh*, "to wake," and signifying one who has awakened to a knowledge of Supreme Truth) is the title given to Gautama Śākyamuni, or "Seer of the Śākyas," who founded the Buddhist doctrine, and whose life will be sketched briefly in the following section. He was a great man and seer of the highest spiritual attainment possible on the earthly plane—a fully enlightened being—but is never regarded as a god, or even as a savior except as he showed us the way to become like him and to unfold our *own* Enlightenment.

In the Theravāda, the Southern Branch of Buddhism, the Buddha, having passed into Final *Nirvāṇa* —transcendent and beyond all ability of the human mind to conceive—as a man, has gone beyond our ken—but lives on in his Teachings and in his ever-present Spirit.

The Northern Branch holds to a similar, but in the Mahāyāna view, a broader concept. In order to convey its meaning, two uses of the word "Buddha"

10

are employed. This necessity, contingent upon the limitations of language, can sometimes lead to mis- understandings.

First, in common with all Buddhists, the Mahā- yāna speaks of "*The* Buddha" (using the article), meaning the fully enlightened man, Gautama, whose Spirit is ever with us in his Teachings. He appears among us in the *Nirmanakāya*, the Emanation Body, or Body of Manifestation, as does every great spir- itually enlightened being. But the Mahāyāna devel- ops the doctrine a step further. Here, and secondly, the word "Buddha," used as a rule *without* the article, signifies the transcendent, spiritual Buddha, or *Essence* of Buddhahood—the Cosmic Buddha- Mind, or Divine Source, the *Dharmakāya,* or Ground of our being—in the essential nature of which every living thing partakes. Hence the dictim: "You, your- self, are Buddha." Man's failure lies in not realizing and demonstrating this truth.

An understanding of these two usages is vital to a comprehension of the Mahāyāna texts. Lack of it has often led, on the part of translators and readers, to the mistaken notion that the *historical* Buddha has been *deified* by Mahāyāna Buddhists. Nothing could be further from the truth. Gautama, the Buddha, embodied and demonstrated this transcendent Buddha-Essence to the fullest degree possible to a human being—but every living creature partakes of it; it is eternally within us, the Buddha-Mind, our real nature, only waiting to be uncovered and unfolded as we strive and evolve toward that Full Enlightenment which Gautama achieved and which is the potential heritage of every living being. There have been other Buddhas in the past, and there will be others yet to come. No particular part of the world is favored in this respect.

LIFE OF THE BUDDHA

The Buddha was born between 2500 and 2600 years ago, the generally accepted date being 563 B.C., at about the same time as the Babylonian captivity of the Jews. His parents were King (or Rājah) Suddhodana of the Śākya Clan (whose territory lay on the borders of what is now Nepal), and his queen Mahāmāyā.

Briefly, the main events of his life are as follows: When Mahāmāyā knew that she was to have a child, she journeyed to Devadaha (her father's home, near Kapilavastu, the capital city of Suddhodana's realm) and the future Buddha was born in the Lumbini

Garden there. Miraculous events attended his birth. The baby was named Siddhārtha, meaning Perfect Fulfillment. Gautama was his family name, and Śākyamuni, or "Sage of the Śākyas," was a later title given to him after his Enlightenment.

It was prophesied at his birth that he would become either a great world ruler, or a great Sage and spiritual Teacher. Naturally his father hoped for the former as the destiny of his heir.

Most of us know the main events of the Buddha's early life, most widely outlined in the literature, so I will not go into further details of them here. Suffice it to say that the young Prince, growing weary of the ceaseless pleasures of palace life provided by his father to shield him from contact with painful realities beyond the palace walls, and thus to keep him as a willing heir to the throne, and learning for the first time of the sorrow, sickness, and death to be found in the world outside, forsook his inheritance at the age of twenty-nine, and quietly bidding farewell to his young wife and child as they slept, set forth into the forest to find Enlightenment and a remedy for the sorrows of the world. These he found after six years of fruitless searching and profitless austerities, while sitting in deep meditation under a fig tree (the Bodhi Tree) at Bodh Gaya in Northern

13

India. He thus became the Buddha, the Fully Enlightened One, whose Teachings have survived and gathered countless followers for more than twenty centuries.

The ministry of the Buddha lasted for forty-five years. He passed into Final *Nirvāṇa* at Kusinagara in 483 B.C., at the age of eighty, having brought peace and Enlightenment to all who truly followed him. As he lay dying to the world, sorrowing disciples and even the forest animals gathered round him. Weeping, Ānanda, his cousin and chief disciple, asked him: "What are we to do without our beloved Master to guide us?" The Buddha, comforting all, replied: "Decay is inherent in all compounded things. Strive unceasingly." These were his final words—all this, remember, five hundred years before the beginning of the Christian era.

HISTORY

Buddhism was heir to the civilization and religion of ancient India as found in the sacred books—the Vedas, Brāhmanas, and Upanishads. But the Buddha was a reformer of the religion of his time—rejecting such things as the popular conception of many gods, excessive ritualism, the caste system within the

Saṅgha, or Brotherhood, the inequality of women, and the power of the priesthood. In Buddhism we find the truest kind of democracy in action.

After the Buddha's death, Buddhism spread far and wide through the teaching of his disciples, and later under the aegis of the great Emperor Āśoka (273-232 B.C.), part of whose commemorative Lion Pillar (one of the many setting forth his edicts) still stands at Sarnath.

Buddhism under Āśoka became the state religion of India, while still honoring and respecting all other religions in the realm. Buddhism has never forced its doctrines on anyone, or waged a religious war for conquest and conversion of non-Buddhists. This is more than can be said for any other religion of which I know. It was by persuasion and example that the religion spread. It was also popular because of its message of equality and brotherhood, its teaching of *unity*, not "separateness," and because it accorded all living things a place on the ladder of evolution and progression toward Enlightenment. Thus "evolution" is not such a modern concept after all!

Later, in the very early centuries of our era, Buddhism divided into the two great Branches of which we have spoken—the Southern (based on

15

the earliest scriptures and placing its emphasis on the Saṅgha, or Religious Order, and on the personal attainment of *Nirvāṇa,* or Ultimate Enlightenment —the *Arhat* ideal—of which the modern Theravāda of Burma, Thailand, Cambodia, Laos, and Ceylon is the heir and surviving sect); and the Northern, or Mahāyāna Branch, where the great Indian Buddhist University of Nālanda (a power in Buddhism for a thousand years) played a leading role in its development. The Mahāyāna is found mainly in Tibet, Nepal, Sikkim, Bhutan, China, Viet Nam, Korea, and Japan, and emphasizes the ideal of the *Bodhisattva*—one who, having attained the last stage preceding Buddhahood, renounces Final *Nirvāṇa,* when he no longer need be reborn in further incarnations—in order voluntarily to return in another birth or births to help and save others. The Bodhisattva represents the *active* force of Buddhahood and, at certain levels, may be any great saint or humanitarian, regardless of his race, religion, national origin, or even awareness of the status he holds.

There may also be spiritual Bodhisattvas functioning in the *Sambhogakāya* or "Heavenly Body of Bliss,"* such as Chenresi (Skt.: Avalokiteśvara; Ch.:

* See p. 55 for a definition of the *Sambhogakāya.*

16

Kwan Yin; Jap.: Kwannon), the Patron Bodhisattva of Tibet, who, though no longer on this earth, still have a deep concern for all living beings and, as way-showers, extend their love and spiritual help to all. The Vow of the Bodhisattva is a dedication of his life to *all* life, to the end that every sentient being may attain Liberation.

This brings to mind a golden image of Avalokiteśvara in my own collection—"Chenresi, the greatly compassionate"—of whom the Dalai Lama is said to be a manifestation. Sitting in the Lotus Posture, in deep meditation, he holds in his folded hands the Sphere of the Essence of Wisdom, and is surrounded by an aura of flame. Everything about this image is a *symbol*, to be understood, not literally, but spiritually and symbolically. The nimbus of flame surrounding him represents Buddhism's fiery energy, as well as the fusion of all things in the fire of Ultimate Truth. Here is the principle of *Integration*, taught in the symbol of light.

In the deepest sense, Chenresi, as does every Bodhisattva, represents some aspect of the Buddha-Mind itself—the reality of the Buddhahood inherent in every being, the ineffable Buddha-nature within each human heart.

Mahāyānists feel that the "Bodhisatta" doctrine,

interpreted in the Theravāda Scriptures as applying to "an aspirant to Buddhahood" and used as a title for the Buddha in the Jātaka Tales of his former incarnations, has come to full flower in the doctrine of the Bodhisattva. This casts no aspersions upon the Buddha himself who, as Mahāsattva (or Great Bodhisattva) prior to his Final Enlightenment under the Bodhi Tree, strove with compassion to alleviate sorrow and to bring Enlightenment to others; and as the Fully Enlightened Buddha, left us and the Bodhisattvas who followed him, with a means of salvation for all time.

All this does not mean that the Theravāda ("The Teaching of the Elders") turns its back upon compassion and help for others, or that the Mahāyāna neglects the spiritual evolution of the individual. It is chiefly a matter of method and emphasis where this point is concerned. But in either case, *practice* is essential. The Mahāyāna holds that *all* good and helpful spiritual teachings, based on the Scriptures and designed for travelers at whatever stage on the Path, are steps toward the Final Teaching, which employs neither ritual, symbol, mantra (invocation), nor any exertive or external practice, but is wholly inward, and of Mind itself. According to Milarepa, Tibet's great poet-saint of the 11th to 12th century, all branches and schools of Buddhism have their value and their function to fulfill (as do all religions) for those of differing inclinations and "wavelengths." He also spoke of sentient beings as his "parents"— for in countless incarnations all beings, at one time or another, have held this relationship to one another. On these grounds he warned against discrimination in any form; he decried clinging to one's own School or religion and condemning others, for he taught that since all Dharmas (spiritual teachings) are equally good, sectarianism only degrades Buddhism and leads to severance from Liberation. This good advice can be pondered not only by Buddhists, but by adherents of every faith.

Later, Buddhism died out in India for many hundreds of years, due to the return of the Brahmin priesthood to power, invasion of the Moslems, and other causes. Only recently has there been a resurgence of Buddhism in India. It was spread to other countries, however, by scholar-monks and pilgrims, either journeying to its source or spreading outward from India by invitation of foreign rulers or to escape persecution there. The Scriptures were carried to other lands and translated from Pāli or Sanskrit into their respective languages at intervals over a long period of time. It is said that today there are some 500,000,000 Buddhists in the world—between one quarter and one third of the world's population.

English translations from the vast literature of Buddhism, begun only within the past hundred years, have now reached sizable proportions; but there is still a tremendous amount of work to be done in the field. It will be many years before we can say that a major portion is available in English for scholars and students in the West. The earlier translations, of fifty or more years ago, in some cases gave a rather inaccurate picture of much of the teaching, depicting it as atheistic, pantheistic, or even nihilistic—whereas in reality it is nothing of the sort. Misunderstanding of terminology and meaning, the difficulty of finding English equivalents for certain words and concepts foreign to Western ways of thinking, even ignorance or prejudice on the part of some of the early translators, have been responsible for much of this. To the Buddhist, "Buddha" defined as "Mind" or "Spirit"—the Cosmic Ground of our being—is both immanent *and* transcendent. Therefore Buddhism, to quote Dr. Arthur W. Hummel, "is not Pantheism, which says that all things are God—and so imprisons God in His universe." To the Buddhist, as we have emphasized before, mat-

20

ter is but another aspect of Spirit—a manifestation, a condensation—relative, transient, in a constant state of flux or becoming, and in the *ultimate* sense, illusory and unreal. Emerson said: "The world is Mind precipitated"; and to quote Sir Sarvepalli Radhakrishnan, "Ultimate Reality sleeps in the stone, breathes in the plant, feels in the animal, and awakes to self-consciousness in man."

This does not mean that Buddhism accepts the doctrine of a personal Deity who created the universe and man at some specific time in the past (for to the Buddhist the universe is beginningless and endless), but that all life is ultimately based upon a completely transcendent and non-material foundation.

DOCTRINES

Before going in greater detail into the Basic Teachings, perhaps a more specific discussion of one or two important terms may be useful.

Enlightenment

"Enlightenment" as used in the Buddhist sense does not refer to the ordinarily understood meaning of the word, that is, to intellectual understanding as conveyed by teachings such as one obtains in school or university, or by the reading and study of books. Buddhist Enlightenment goes far deeper than this without, of course, discounting the value of intellectual thought and study at their own level. Enlightenment as the Buddhist sees it is based upon *intuitive understanding* gained through right living at *every* level, and by *meditation,* which takes one through and beyond the limits of discursive thinking and awakens the faculties of the inner, intuitive mind. This practice can be developed into a continuous substratum of thought even as we go about our daily activities. It leads to spiritual illumination and an ultimate realization of the meaning and purpose of life. It is not done to change the *conditions* of life (although Karmic effects will follow if we are not too concerned about them), but gives us a different attitude *toward* life—and so furthers detachment without loss of love, and equanimity in the face of every circumstance. In Western terminology, "Cosmic Consciousness" might be said to approach this experience, but the effects of Buddhist Enlightenment, even at a minor or partial level, can be of lasting benefit and of *practical application in every moment of daily living.* Enlightenment in varying

degrees will come to all of us with the practices that
the Buddha taught, and· *Ultimate* Enlightenment,
or *Parinirvāṇa*, is the goal of all Buddhist practice.

Nirvāṇa

Nirvāṇa is not, as many have been falsely led to
believe, a state of "nothingness," or the goal of
escapism. It is neither extinction, nor annihilation, of
anything that is *real;* nor is it ascending to some
eternal heaven. Only those things which are evil and
illusory are extinguished in *Nirvāṇa,* for *Nirvāṇa* is
not a place, but a *state of consciousness*—of liberation from all ignorance, greed, selfishness, dualistic
thinking, and belief in an eternally existing ego; of
liberation from materialistic ideas, thoughts, beliefs,
and ties—the extinction of all craving for and belief
in the absolute reality of material things, as well as
of mental objects in the *Sambhogakāya,* i.e., heavens,
hells, Buddhas and Bodhisattvas as *discrete entities,*
i.e., of everything conceivable by the dualistic, con-
ceptualizing, and discursive human mind. As the
extinction of "Karmically conditioned existence" (of
life conditioned by the causes and effects we set up
by our own actions), it is liberation from the need to
return to an earthly existence (the only state in
which more "schooling" is possible, unless it be that

23

of *Sukhāvatī*, the Paradise, or Pure Land envisioned and aspired to by the Shin and Jōdo Schools—of which more later), release from continued rebirths and from the Cycle of Birth-and-Death. *Nirvāṇa* is Enlightenment itself, and need not be reserved for some future life but is realizable now, in this very life, though improbable for most of us in our present state of development.

Finally, *Parinirvāṇa*, the Ultimate Enlightenment achieved by the Buddha himself at his final passing from human ken, is beyond all conception, for here every human concept is destroyed in the eternal Plenum-Void—the ineffable Goal of all Buddhist experience.

Dharma

"Dharma," for which there is no exact over-all equivalent in the English language, has many meanings. For our present purpose, however, "The Law as exemplified in the Buddhist Teachings," or "The Universal, Cosmic Law," are the most important. Thus we speak of "The Dharma" as the Teachings of the Buddha or as the Spiritual Law of Life. Uncapitalized, and usually in the plural, "dharmas" mean things, thoughts, elements, or concepts in general. For a fuller exposition of this subject, see references.[3]

Basically, the Buddha's teachings concern the cause of sorrow, and how to think and act in ways that bring release from it. *The Middle Way* between self-indulgence and asceticism (and also between "The Opposites": real and unreal, "is" and "is not," etc., to be discussed later in connection with the Mādhyamika philosophy of Nāgārjuna, pp. 50-51), *The Four Noble Truths, The Eight-fold Path* leading to release from suffering, and *The Twelve-fold Chain, or Circle of Dependent Origination*—the Cycle of Birth-and-Death (beginning with spiritual ignorance and ending with death and rebirth) are the foundation stones of all Buddhist philosophy and practice.

Of *Sorrow* the Buddha said: "In the world there are the sorrows of truth, of death, of disease, and of old age; the sorrow of loving that which cannot be obtained, of hating that which cannot be avoided, and the thirst for life. These are the sacred truths of sorrow. Here also is the truth of the destruction of sorrow. It is the quenching of thirst by the quenching of desire."

Of *The Middle Way* the Buddha said: "There are two extremes which we must avoid. The life of carnal pleasure is ignoble, contrary to the spiritual life,

25

unworthy, and vain. But a life of austerities is also sorrowful, unworthy, and vain. Between these two extremes, the perfect is the Middle Way. For this path brings rest, illumination, and *Nirvāṇa*. Here lies Truth which brings victory over sorrow. This is the Eight-fold Path that leads to [Enlightenment]. For there are Four Great Truths":

✤ All life knows sorrow
> (that is, sorrow in the widest possible sense: pain, anxiety, frustration, grief, loss, and all the ills that afflict mankind)

✤ This sorrow has a cause
> (spiritual ignorance, and thus false ideas, which in turn give rise to selfishness, grasping, and desire)

✤ Sorrow can be brought to an end

✤ The way to bring sorrow to an end. This way is:

The Noble Eight-fold Path:

✤ The steps leading to Wisdom
> RIGHT UNDERSTANDING, or KNOWLEDGE
> (the first step, and the basis from which all others must follow, or we will go astray)
> RIGHT ASPIRATION

(the will to attain, based on self-discipline and inner, intuitive vision)

❀ The steps leading to Virtue

RIGHT SPEECH

(Shun gossip, slander, abuse of others, and foolish talk; be truthful and kind in all you say.)

RIGHT ACTION, OR CONDUCT

(Let each action be guided by the inner law of Love, Compassion, and Wisdom.)

RIGHT LIVELIHOOD

(Engage in work which injures no one, man or any other living creature.)

❀ The steps leading to Concentration

RIGHT EFFORT

(Apply one's strength and energy, with understanding, to wise and useful purposes.)

RIGHT MINDFULNESS

(in every activity of life)

RIGHT MEDITATION, OR CONTEMPLATION

It is here that a word must be said about one of the greatest foundation stones of Buddhist practice, i.e., *Satipaṭṭhāna,* or *The Way of Mindfulness* enunciated by the Buddha himself, and based on the

Seventh Step in the Path toward the extinction of suffering. It is one of the two great divisions, or "Ways" of Buddhist meditation practice, the first being the Development of Tranquillity (through cultivation of the intuitive mind), and the second, Mindfulness, being the Development of Insight (through discipline and training of the discursive mind). For those of us living in this modern world of stress, confusions, and distractions, and for the majority of modern-day temperaments (particularly in the West), the Way of Mindfulness is undoubtedly the better method with which to begin our meditational training although, ideally, the attainment of Tranquillity through awakening of the intuitive mind comes first—and for *suitable temperaments* will precede it. But the "separateness" of these two paths is only apparent—their unity will be experienced with continued practice—for one leads to the other; they merge in the same Goal. But here it is *Satipaṭṭhāna* that we shall discuss.

Without Mindfulness, leading to awareness and Insight into all we see, feel, think, and do, all other efforts toward the unfolding of Enlightenment could fall by the wayside. Nyanaponika Thera, in his comprehensive handbook of mental and meditational training, "The Heart of Buddhist Meditation, Based

28

on the Buddha's Way of Mindfulness,"[4] divides *Satipaṭṭhāna* into several steps, i.e., Bare Attention; Clear Comprehension; The Four Objects of Mindfulness (body, feelings, state of mind, mental contents); and The Culture of Mind.

The initial exercise consists of Bare Attention to bodily movements (breathing, touching-sitting, walking)—especially to the rise and fall of the abdomen as one breathes. Later one takes up, one by one, the other bodily, mental, and emotional processes as they occur at any given moment. No analysis or thoughts *about* them are allowed to intrude—one simply takes note of them. Even distractions, such as noise or confusion, can be used as objects of Bare Attention and so as meditational aids.

Clear Comprehension—of purpose, suitability, and reality (non-delusion)—is the next step. These two basics in themselves form a powerful meditation practice; and when continued for ever-lengthening periods of time without a break in attention (or without an unnoticed break), form a disciplined mental training, a strengthening of the powers of concentration, and development of the mind into a clear and subtle instrument.

In the Culture of Mind, *Satipaṭṭhāna*, as a message of self-help, teaches self-reliance, simplicity, naturalness, adaptability, and thoughtfulness; and results in the improvement of every-day work and living and in the harmonious functioning of the mind itself.

A lucid account of this training as given in a Burmese monastery and undergone by an English disciple will be found in the enlightening little book by Rear Admiral E. H. Shattock.[5] Here, a concentrated period of training free of outside duties and distractions was experienced under a meditation Master—the ideal way if one is to make rapid progress. For most of us however, who do not have such an opportunity, *self*-training under guidance can be vastly helpful if earnestly adhered to. For this purpose Nyanaponika Thera's book, mentioned above, is unsurpassed. In addition to an outline of the specific steps and methods, with further comment on *Satipaṭṭhāna* as practiced in Burma, he includes an Anthology of Relevant Texts translated from both Pāli and Sanskrit, with Commentaries, and extracts from the Mahāyāna literature. It goes without saying that the words of the Buddha as found in the Pāli Canon occupy the most prominent place, but the Mahāyāna Masters are far from neglected. This quotation from Nāgārjuna is a case in point:

The Four Foundations of Mindfulness have unmistakably been shown as the Only Way trodden by the Buddhas. Guard them at all times! Negligence in them makes all efforts useless, and it is the persevering practice of them that is called "concentration of mind" (*Samādhi*).

The earnest student will find this book of inestimable value.[4]

The last step in the Eight-fold Path—Right Meditation, or Contemplation, is the culmination of all that preceded it. Tranquillity and Illumination arise therefrom. Its practice is indispensable, as the Buddha reiterated again and again, if we are to release the inner, intuitive mind from the fetters of the ordinary (and outer) discursive mind. There are many degrees of this absorption, and many techniques for attaining it—some of the highest nature achieved only after long training, practice, and self-discipline; but there is one thing even the beginner can do. Suggested by the Buddha himself, it is known as the *Mettā*, or Loving-kindness Meditation. Sitting quietly and at some appropriate part of the day, alone and in a quiet place, shut out all thoughts of the every-day world and its problems, and mentally broadcast love, friendliness, and goodwill to every sentient being, including oneself— North, South, East, and West in turn, and to the zenith above and the nadir below. There is power

31

in thought—we *are* our thoughts—and every good thought broadcast to the world and to the beings in it adds that much weight in the balance against evil and illusion. From this first step others will follow naturally—evenness of breath, relaxation of body and mind with no loss of awareness, tranquillity, and intuitive realization of THAT which is *beyond* self —through the surrender of self.

Thus in the Seventh and Eighth Steps shown we have been given the two great modes of meditation—a perfect balance in accord with the needs of the human mind—the two unsurpassed Ways which, together, will lead to Final Liberation.

Contemplative meditation will be discussed further in subsequent chapters.

The Refuges

Buddhism also teaches that of paramount necessity to the practicing Buddhist are the Three Refuges, or Venerations, which he takes upon becoming a Buddhist and mindfully and reverently repeats thereafter—morning, evening, before every meditation period, and whenever else he can. Thus they dwell and work as leaven in his heart, even when he is not consciously thinking of them.

❀ "I take refuge in the Buddha"

(that is, refuge and reliance—with inexpressible gratitude, love, and veneration—in the Buddha, the man, the Enlightened One and, to all Buddhists, the greatest human being of this world age, who showed us the Path to release from suffering; plus refuge—from the standpoint of the Mahāyāna—in the spiritual Principle, or *Essence* of Buddhahood, which Gautama embodied to the full, and which permeates the universe and every sentient being in it)

❀ "I take refuge in the Dharma"

(in the Spiritual Law, or the Buddhist Teachings)

❀ "I take refuge in the Saṅgha"

(specifically, in the Buddhist religious Order; more widely, and in the Mahāyāna Tradition, in the Buddhist Community as a whole)

The *Tibetan* Buddhist takes a fourth:

❀ "I take refuge in the Guru"

(for his Teacher, next to the Buddha himself, is his refuge and his guide)

Two other important concomitants of the Basic Teaching are:

❀ *The Six (or Ten) Pāramitās,* or Perfections of the Bodhisattva

> (fulfilled by the Buddha in his former lives), the first six being:

>> Charity, Discipline, Patience, Diligence, Inner Vision through Meditation, and Wisdom

> The last four, amplifications of *Prajñā,* or Wisdom, are:

>> Skillful Means of Teaching, Power over Obstacles, Spiritual Aspiration, and Knowledge

❀ *The Five Precepts*

> (extremely important in Buddhist practice, and taken by all laymen. Monks assume many more than these.)

>> To kill no living thing
>> To cheat no one, nor steal
>> To commit no adultery
>> To tell no lies, nor deceive
>> To take no intoxicating liquors or drugs that confuse the mind

> Sometimes four more are added:

>> To speak no slander, nor hold profane talk
>> Not to covet or give way to anger
>> To have no foolish doubts
>> To abide by all that is right and true

As one can clearly see, the Precepts are very similar to the Ten Commandments of the Hebrew-Christian Tradition, but there is one important difference. Here we are not *commanded* to do anything under threat of punishment from any outside Power. *The Law of Karma* takes care that eventually and inevitably good follows good thoughts and actions, and evil, evil ones. The desire to live rightly must come from *within ourselves* through right understanding, aims, and effort. Basically, Buddhism is a "do it yourself" religion. The Masters and Teachers can show us the way, help us to overcome spiritual ignorance, but no one, not even the Buddha himself, can do it for us. Vicarious atonement, as such, has no place in the Buddhist teachings. By the same token, there is no teaching of sin punishable by an arbitrary Power outside of ourselves. "Buddhism recognizes no original sin in man, save those results of his own past causes which have not yet ripened."[6] Hence the Buddhist saying noted before: "We are not punished *for* our sins but *by* them."

Buddhists understand the "Divine" not as a personal, anthropomorphic God, but as Mind, Principle, Ultimate Truth, Spiritual Law, Thatness, or Thusness. Actually no name can be given to Ultimate Truth because it transcends all name and form; but because on the human level we must use language, in teaching we resort to these terms. They only approximate intellectually that which, in the end, must be realized intuitively within each human heart.

Buddhism, particularly the Mahāyāna, is not unaware, however, that there are many people whose natures require a more personal approach—through simple but perceptive faith; through ritual and ceremony; or through the "other power" way of devotion to and reliance on a more personal aspect or manifestation of the Buddha-Spirit, as in the "Pure Land" (*Sukhāvatī*) School of Amitābha (Amida), the Buddha of Life and Light and the personification of Compassion, who dwells in the "Western Paradise"—really not a distant place, but in *Ultimate Reality* that Pure Land within the heart of man himself. These ways are all good, for they are simply different paths to the same goal—like the spokes of a wheel all leading to the hub, or the trails up a mountain all leading to the heights.

In the Mahāyāna it is taught, therefore, that the merits and Compassion of the Buddhas and Bodhisattvas can save sentient beings from their own spiritual ignorance (*Avidyā*, non-awareness), and thus help them to overcome the effects of even Karma itself. In the final analysis, however, it is only the approach and methods that differ. The goal—Enlightenment—is the same for all(The Essence of Buddhism is never lost in the multiplicity of its methods and sects.)

Finally, a word should be said about the *Nidānas* —the Twelve-fold Chain, or Circle, of Dependent Origination, the Causal Wheel, the Cycle of Birth-and-Death by which a being comes into existence. This is referred to many times in the early Scriptures as well as in the later ones, and is the philosophical basis for the whole Doctrine of the Buddha. This "Dependent Arising"—the principle of conditionality, relativity, and interdependence—is expressed most succinctly in the short scriptural formula:

> When this is, that is
> This arising, that arises
> When this is not, that is not
> This ceasing, that ceases.

The Buddha, in answer to the questions of Kassapa, outlined the formula thus:

Dependent on ignorance (of the true nature of things), arise volitional or Karma formations.

Dependent on volitional-formations, arises (rebirth) consciousness.

Dependent on consciousness, arises mentality-materiality (psychophysical combinations).

Dependent on mentality-materiality, arises the sixfold base (the five physical senses with consciousness as the sixth).

Dependent on the sixfold base, arises contact.

Dependent on contact, arises feeling.

Dependent on feeling, arises craving.

Dependent on craving, arises clinging.

Dependent on clinging arises the process of becoming.

Dependent on the process of becoming, arise aging and death, sorrow, lamentation, pain, grief, and despair. Thus does this whole mass of suffering arise. (This is called the Noble Truth of the Arising of Suffering or *dukkha*.)

Through the entire cessation of ignorance, cease volitional formations; through the cessation of volitional formations, consciousness . . . (etc.). Thus does this whole mass of suffering cease. (This is called the Noble Truth of the Cessation of Suffering.)[7]

Because each of these factors is both conditioned and conditioning, no first cause is accepted by Buddhism.

Christmas Humphreys comments: "As [the *Nidānas* comprise a circle, or wheel] there is no starting point, but as Ignorance is the primary root of existence, and because its complete removal is essential for escape from rebirth, it is usually placed first."[6]

The Wheel ends with the formula: "Such is the uprising of this entire body of evil."*

One further brief comment—on the relationship of the Law of Karma to the resulting Birth-and-Death Cycle—for they are inseparable. According to Buddhism no one life (with rare exceptions) is sufficient to work out all the effects of the causes we set up through our own past thoughts and deeds. Until Enlightenment is achieved, every one of us is subject to rebirth, either here or elsewhere, under whatever conditions we have shaped for ourselves in this life or in past ones. Therefore every day and every hour of every day is "Judgment Day" to the Buddhist. Karma does not necessarily wait until a future life to manifest itself. According to the *Abhidhamma,* one of the great Scriptures of early Buddhism, "birth" and "death" take place simultaneously every moment. It is in *this* sense that the Christ spoke of being "born anew." Our "fate" in the present is not a matter of chance, or "luck," but is merely the result, good or bad, of what we have done in the past; and what we do today will affect or determine our tomorrows. Therefore Karma may catch up with us in this very life, often does, or may be deferred until some future one.

* For a further discussion of the *Nidānas,* see pp. 56-59.

As I have mentioned before, it is our characters as we have shaped them for good or evil that are reborn in another body and personality; the transient, personal ego is only *relatively* real. Buddhism does not accept the doctrine of "an immortal, unchanging entity, or soul, created by a Deity, the destiny of which may be eternal happiness [in heaven] or eternal misery [in hell] according to the deeds of the personality it ensouls."[6] Neither "heaven" nor "hell" is a permanent condition, says the Buddhist, nor are they localities—either above or below (regardless of popular beliefs)—but are *states of consciousness* lasting only until the Karma which produced them is worked out or exhausted. "Soul," therefore, is a term usually avoided by Buddhists (except in the most relative, transient sense), as is the term "God," to avoid all misconceptions. According to Buddhism, the "being" or "ego" is an ever-changing *aggregate,* or bundle of characteristics composed of five elements, or *Skandhas*: the physical body and its senses; feelings or sensations; emotional reactions or volition; perceptions leading to memory; and consciousness. Take all these away, and what have you left? Certainly nothing that can be called a "self." Therefore it is the life-force arising from the interaction of these five elements and shaped by our own actions and experiences in the phenomenal worlds—past or present—[as it becomes] "more and more enlightened by following the Path, or more degraded by departing from it,"[6] that is carried on into other births. Thus rebirth may be compared to the lighting of a new candle from the flame of an old one: the *flame* goes on, but the *candle* is consumed. Each new flame arises and takes its character from the preceding one, but is not identical with it; nor is the candle the same.

So we see that the Buddha-nature—Spirit, Mind —alone is real, unchanging and eternal. But all of us, as manifestations of this Spirit, have Buddhahood inherent within us. As Buddhism teaches, it is possible to attain, or rather to *unfold* it in one lifetime— but improbable for most of us. The Buddha's life was the culmination of a long upward climb through many experiences and many lives in the past. "It is the wholeness of the evolutionary process of being born again and again," a discerning Buddhist has said, "no matter in what walk of life, striving each time for greater perfection or perfection in another aspect of being—in contrast to the process of being born only once, as a man striving to go to heaven or avoid hell—that would seem to offer the great hopefulness of an endless scale of values, the immense joy of *being alive more and more.*" This is an essential part of the Buddhist world-view.

It is a little-known fact, but verifiable in the records, that the Christian Church held to the doctrine of rebirth until the year 553, when it was rejected by the 2nd Council of Constantinople (as detracting from the power of the priesthood to "remit sins," according to some accounts), one third of the participating bishops voting for it, and two thirds against it.*

SUMMARY

To recapitulate: Gautama, the Buddha, was unique in this world-age, though not the only Buddha in the world's long history. He was the successor to previous Buddhas of past ages and the forerunner of others to come.

According to Buddhism, life is beginningless and endless, not a "creation" brought into being by a Deity at some specific time in the past. Whatever has a beginning must have an ending, says the Buddhist; but life is eternal—it flows, is a flux; manifestation is

---

* Another record refers to an earlier rejection taking place at the Council of Alexandria in the year 550.

continuous, and the only rule is *Anicca,* change—the impermanence of all compounded things. Truth, Ultimate Reality, alone is unchanging; all else is relative, in process of becoming, subject to the Cycle of Birth-and-Death. *Nirvāna*—Supreme Enlightenment—is liberation from this Karmically conditioned existence —a perfected state of consciousness where all ignorance, delusion, and worldly desire are destroyed. *Nirvāna* is not extinction of anything that is *real,* nor annihilation—only that of craving for and belief in the ultimate reality of the personal ego-soul and material things.

Although in his final earthly appearance in the *Nirmānakāya** a Buddha may resemble an ordinary man, such an event as the presence of a Buddha among us is rare. There are Bodhisattvas, however, about us and with us even today. The Buddha had many lives as a Bodhisattva behind him; and his Buddhahood was the result of continuous striving through innumerable previous lives—performing saintly and helpful deeds for the benefit of all living beings. Many of these lives are recounted for us in the Jātaka Tales—remembrances of past incarnations told by the Buddha to his disciples at Śrāvastī, and recorded by the scholar Ārya Śūra. According to the

* See p. 55 for a definition of the *Nirmānakāya.*

bent of the reader, these Tales may be taken literally, or may be understood symbolically as an epitome, a prophetic and microcosmic panorama, illumined by the destiny of a single being, of the history and evolution of the entire human race.

Thus the Buddha Śākyamuni became a perfected being, a true Buddha, in his final incarnation on earth. He left us with this simple summary of all his teachings:

> Cease to do evil, do good; purify the
> heart and mind;
> This is the teaching of all the Buddhas.

So we see that Buddhism is not given exclusively for the benefit of one group of people, or for any historical period, or for any geographical place. Nor is it a "foreign" and "exotic" thing of merely passing and theoretical interest. It is as modern as tomorrow, because it is *ageless*. The Teachings of Gautama are as applicable today—to modern man, struggling in the hectic and materialistic civilization he has created for himself, dominated by technology and the quest for gain, and careless of the destruction of resources and beauty in the natural world—as they ever were in any other culture or any other time in the past.

Insofar as we can forget, even for a moment, our preoccupation with the race for money and status, with desire for more and better possessions, with concern for self and indifference to others, and with the will to power—and concentrate on the true and lasting values of life, to that extent will we find true peace, and release from the tensions, frustrations, and afflictions that beset us on every hand; to that extent will we find the Path to Enlightenment, and the greatest happiness we have ever known.

2

ORIGINS, DOCTRINES AND SIGNIFICANCE OF THE MAHĀYĀNA[8]

Although much of the origin and rise of the early Mahāyāna is shrouded in the mists of time, we do know certain historical facts, and first of all it is these facts which I shall try to outline here—reviewing what we have learned of the origins of this great Branch of the Buddha Dharma whose followers number in the millions, principally in the northern countries of Asia and now in many parts of the Western world.

Because the Mahāyāna is dynamic and positive, full of variety, and remarkably adaptable, without departing from its basic foundations, to differing times, cultures, and levels of understanding, it appeals to many peoples throughout the world. Because it makes no distinction in status, as potential Buddhas, between one race of men and another, between monk and layman, between young and old, and comes into no essential conflict with modern science, it is particularly appealing to the Western mind. Coomaraswamy has said, "The development of the Mahāyāna is in fact the overflowing of Buddhism from the limits of order into the life of the world. . . ."[9] It is this quality which distinguishes it and, where science is concerned, all of Buddhism from every other religion of which I know.

The elements of the Mahāyāna are derived principally from the following sources:

- *From India*: Evolving in its homeland from a basic heritage of all the Buddha's teachings, its metaphysical, philosophical, psychological, and mystical elements came into flower there.
- *From China*: Following its migration to that land, the Mahāyāna absorbed the relationalistic and humanist elements indigenous to China—fostered by Confucian and Taoist influences—and evolved the Ch'an (Zen) teachings, inspired by the 6th century Indian monk, Bodhidharma, as a revolt against old, formalized rituals and practices which had developed in the course of time.

47

❀ *From Japan*: In Japan the poetical and utilitarian aspects of the Mahāyāna developed more fully, closely interwoven with the unorthodox and iconoclastic elements of Zen which it had brought with it from China.

❀ *From Tibet*: Lastly, Tantric Tibet contributed its adjustments as well, developing its own *upāya* (means, methods) and techniques fully as much as the Chinese and Japanese did.*

With all this, the basic principles of Gautama's teachings remain common to all Schools and sects, both Northern and Southern. Thus the fundamental unity of Buddhism has always been preserved as the great world religion and Way of Life that it is.

The Mahāyāna, according to its tenets, while an early flowering from the original "seed," the Pāli Canon, is also an evolution of the profoundest nature. Because no texts were written down until long after the Buddha's time, it accords equal authenticity to the Sanskrit texts as to those written in Pāli, although it is generally conceded that the Pāli Canon is the older. However, exact dates are difficult to come by,

* For an account of these developments, see Chapter 3, "The Tibetan Vajrayāna," pp. 83-86.

and some of the Sanskrit Sūtras may well lay claim to comparable antiquity.

To go back nearly 2500 years, we know that the Buddha, upon his *Parinirvāna* (final *Nirvāna*) in 483 B.C., had appointed no successor to himself, but at the last had replied to the inquiries of his sorrowing disciples: "Let the Teachings be your guide." Thus, for the following 200-odd years the hearts, minds, and memories of his disciples were the repositories for these Teachings.

However, even the best of human intentions and memories (not to mention individual idiosyncrasies and interpretations) can be fallible, so over the years the wise leaders of ensuing generations called a number of Great Councils, the First not long after the Buddha's *Parinirvāna*, to stabilize the Doctrine.

The Second Council was held at Vaiśālī some 100 years later, and the Third, under the aegis of the great Buddhist king, Aśoka, took place at Pātaliputra ca. 240 B.C. Here the Canon was fixed, but nothing was written down until the 1st century B.C. in Ceylon, when a Fourth Great Council was held.

Nevertheless and in spite of all efforts at stabilization, between the 4th century B.C. and the 4th century A.D. (during which time the disputed Council of King Kanishka took place in A.D. 70), eighteen sects arose, the three most important being:

❀ The *Sarvāstivādins* (3rd century B.C.), who taught that everything of which man is aware by means of the physical senses is real—that is, the empirical and practical view or, as defined in the later, Mahāyāna doctrine of Nāgārjuna, *Relative Truth.*

❀ The *Mahāsanghikas* (1st century, A.D.), who taught that nothing of which man is aware by means of the senses is real—that is, the mystical view or, in the later, Mahāyāna doctrine of Nāgārjuna, *Ultimate Truth.*

❀ The *Theravādins,* who adhered closely to the original Canon fixed in the reign of King Aśoka, together with the Buddha's words as recorded therein during the 1st century B.C. Here emphasis was placed on knowledge, i.e., on the exoteric, pragmatic, ethical, and philosophical view.

Of the original eighteen sects, only the Theravāda survived as such; but the Sarvāstivādins and the Mahāsanghikas were the forerunners of the Mahāyāna, which, after that time, followed two directions:

The Logical School (the Mādhyamika, or Middle

Doctrine) of Nāgārjuna (2nd century A.D.) and

The psychologically oriented School (the Yogā-cāra) of Asangha and Vasubandhu (4th century A.D.).

The Mādhyamika was founded "to harmonize rival doctrines on the nature of Reality" (i.e., all is real *vs.* nothing is real) by its doctrine of Relative *vs.* Absolute Truth, both based on Śūnyatā, or Void-ness—"the nonexistence of things-in-themselves on which so much stress is rightly laid in early Buddhism,"[9] that is, nothing concrete is lasting or has "selfhood" apart from other things.

The Yogācāra emphasized the Mind-Only, or Consciousness-Only doctrine—"A teaching of subjective idealism, not as a speculative belief but as the product of spiritual experience."[6] The Yogācāra also developed the doctrine of the Ālayavijñāna, or Store-consciousness—in one sense akin to the Collective Unconscious of Jung. Here, according to some Schools, memories of the individual (in this or other incarnations), of the race, and of all life are stored. On the other side of the coin, the Ālayavijñāna is also regarded as the storehouse of unexpended Karmic causes.

Śūnyatā, or Voidness— sometimes known as the "Plenum-Void" because from it all things are manifested although it does not consist of them—underlies all "the psychological terms of the Yogācāra School."[6] This Plenum-Void may be thought of as the Unborn, Uncreated, Infinite—the Absolute—transcending everything, finite or infinite, conceivable by the human mind.

It was the Mādhyamika and Yogācāra Schools, together, that brought about a systemization of the Mahāyāna teachings. Śūnyatā developed logically, and intuitively, from Buddhist experience, as an expression of the doctrines of Anatta, or Anātman, that is, of no ego-soul or permanently existing self, and of Anicca, transience—"the eternal flux of becoming . . . the very essence of Mahāyāna teaching," as Christmas Humphreys has said in his Buddhism.[10] He goes on to say: "All religious experience has found . . . that when self is exhausted there remains but the Plenum-Void, however that experience may be named." In the Mahāyāna, this doctrine gave birth to the Prajñāpāramitā literature, based on Nāgārjuna's Mādhyamika and compiled from then on over the next 1000 years.

Of all this literature, most famous are the Diamond (or Diamond-cutter) Sūtra and the Heart Sūtra—the latter, the shortest of all, being "the most remarkable epitome of the 'Wisdom which has gone

Beyond,' and one of the greatest scriptures in the world."[6] (The Heart Sūtra is recited daily in all Zen monasteries.)

This Sūtra illustrates the method of negation and paradox, in which "reason is used to destroy itself,"[10] employed in Buddhism to convey a realization of something inexpressible in words. Here the basic impact is that the Dharma-Truth can be realized only through intuition, not by the discursive intellect, which must be silenced if we are to free the intuitive mind.

Lao-tsu, one of the great Sages of early China, founder of Taoism, and a contemporary of both Gautama and Confucius, said: "Those who speak, do not know; those who know, cannot speak." But Lao-tsu also said that the Tao (Ultimate Reality) as *expressed*, i.e., as manifested in the visible world, is the Mother of all created things.

With these statements the Mahāyāna would certainly agree, for they illustrate the distinction between Absolute Truth and Relative Truth—one of its most fundamental doctrines.

The often-discussed Bodhisattva doctrine of the Mahāyāna—a development from the original concept of the "Bodhisatta," or aspirant to Buddahood, as we have indicated before—simply expressed the ideal of salvation for others before self. It is based in part on the doctrine of the Transferrence of Merit.* The Bodhisattva's Vow (the Vow of Avalokiteśvara)† has been succinctly expressed by Govinda as follows: "Whatever be the highest perfection of the human mind, may I realize it for the benefit of all that lives."[11] The Bodhisattva foregoes *Nirvāṇa* until he has fulfilled this Vow.

The Vow to save all sentient beings is not impossible of fulfillment because all life functions as "thought-waves" in Cosmic Mind, and so the thoughts and actions of any being have power to affect all other beings. We will discuss this aspect of universal Karma in the next Section on "Destiny" (see pp. 67-68). It is therefore in Mind, in higher Consciousness, that such "Grace" can be bestowed and shared.

The *Trikāya*, or "Three Bodies of Buddha" doctrine is also implicit in the Mahāyāna. The three "Bodies" may be stated as follows:

The *Dharmakāya*:

> the "Body of the Law," or "Essence Body," i.e., the Logos, the Absolute.

---

* *Parināmanā.* See pp. 68-69.
† See pp. 16-17, 69-70.

❀ The *Sambhogakāya*:

the "Body of Bliss"—the spiritual and dynamic manifestation of the *Dharmakāya*. That in which the Buddha-Mind, or Essence, communicates with the Bodhisattvas.

❀ The *Nirmānakāya*:

the "Emanation Body" as it appears in the ordinary *Samsāric* world; the individual Buddhic or Bodhisattvic incarnation, i.e., the great spiritual Teacher or religious Leader, the Saint. At this high level, specific religions in the framework of which the *Nirmānakāya* appears do not signify.

Of course none of these "Bodies" is to be understood in the ordinary sense. The *Nirmānakāya*, while manifesting on the physical plane and partaking of its characteristics, transcends the "ordinary" physical body such as yours and mine. As the visible body of a Buddha or Bodhisattva, it is "tuned to a higher key." Nor is the *Nirmānakāya* confined to one unique, historical event as in Christianity. There have been many great incarnations (Buddhas and Bodhisattvas) on earth in the past, and there will be others yet to come wherever and whenever the need of sentient beings is greatest. The Buddha and all of the world's great spiritual leaders and "saviors" appeared among us in the *Nirmānakāya,* regardless of the milieu in which they manifested. There are Bodhisattvic incarnations, too, at different levels and with differing spiritual functions, with us even today regardless of race or religion or even, in many cases, awareness of the status they hold; and there are spiritual Bodhisattvas such as Avalokiteśvara functioning in the *Sambhogakāya,* who may or may not ever have lived on earth. It is in the *Sambhogakāya* that they are aware of each other—in states of higher consciousness (the Heavens of Form) sometimes touched by us in deep meditation. The Formless Heavens are beyond comprehension of the ordinary discursive mind and can be realized through spiritual intuition only.

The *Dharmakāya,* the "Body of the Law," is even more than this, for here "Dharma" signifies ". . . *Tattva,* or 'Suchness,' *Śūnya,* 'the void' or 'abyss,' *Nirvāṇa,* 'the eternal liberty,' . . . *Bodhi,* 'wisdom,' *Prajñā,* 'divine knowledge,' *Tathāgata-garbha,* 'the womb of those who attain.' "[9]

Finally, this chapter should not close without a further brief discussion of the Twelve *Nidānas,* or Wheel of Dependent Origination enunciated by the Buddha in the *Saṃyutta-nikāya* (see pp. 37-39), as they play as vital a part in the Mahāyāna Schools as in all other Buddhist Schools and sects.

The *Nidānas* fall into three main divisions: those arising from Karmic conditions in a previous existence, those arising in the present life, and those immediate causes and conditions which bring about future suffering. They may be outlined as follows:

❀ *In a previous existence:*
>Spiritual ignorance, non-awareness, delusion, resulting in Misperceptions
>>(misdirected thoughts and will, belief in a separate "self," which create Karma, or actions affecting future existence)

❀ *In the present life:*
>Consciousness
>>(the first subliminal consciousness in a new life at conception)

>Next:

>Name and form, or mind and body
>>(in the embryo before the sense organs begin to function)

>Then:

>Awakening of the sense organs; and by means of them Contact

(with things outside of oneself—objects, sights, sounds)

Cooperation of these organs and consciousness begins, resulting in Sensations

(emotions or feeling, including the sexual instinct, creating new Karma) because of

Craving, or thirst for life, which in turn leads to Attachment

(clinging to things, possessions, persons, and the activities of life) resulting in

Coming to be

(various consciously motivated acts and the desire to remain in the round of earthly existence) leading to

❀ *In the future:*

Rebirth, or re-existence, and a new life

(followed by old age, suffering, decay, and death all over again)

Thus in Buddhism generally, conditioned life (*Saṃsāra*) is seen as a continual flux, impermanent, based on Ignorance, and real only in a relative sense.

These are the spokes of the Wheel of the *Nidānas,* whatever the order in which they are considered. Other arrangements are possible, as this is a continuous process, but Ignorance is at the root of all.

From Ignorance rises the thought of "I"—of an enduring, personal self—whereas all we know or can perceive—even our ego—is transitory; there exists but a *becoming*, a succession of instants of consciousness. There are processes (and our ego is part of the "process"), but no static and eternally existing "things." From the thought of ME and MINE arise the "Three Fires" of hatred, lust, and illusion—inseparable from sorrow. The cure, as the Buddha taught, is the removal of the conditions which maintain them. It is Enlightenment—the destruction of Ignorance—and the acquisition of a different attitude toward life, which cannot be described—only experienced. It is Enlightenment alone which can free us from the Wheel of Birth-and-Death.

In the iconography of Tibet, the six-spoked "Wheel of Life," in the form of a Maṇḍala (a pictorial diagram symbolizing the Universe and used in ritual, meditation, and invocation), depicting after-death states of consciousness as well as present ones, is most graphically portrayed. Here are represented the six realms of *Saṃsāra* in which the Cycle of Birth-and-Death, endlessly repeated, takes place. Here Yama, Judge of the Dead and King of the Law, holds before us the six-spoked Wheel in the form of a mirror—not to pronounce judgment but as the mirror of Conscience in which every man may judge himself.

Pictorially represented between the spokes are the six forms of unenlightened existence, i.e., *Devas*, or gods; men; warring Titans (anti-gods), or *Asuras*; *Pretas*, "hungry ghosts," or restless spirits; denizens of Hell; and animals. Yama, as an emanation of Amitābha, the Buddha of Life and Light, in the form of Avalokiteśvara, with infinite compassion descends into all the *saṃsāric* worlds, even into Hell, and with the power of the Mirror of Knowledge and so of Conscience, transmutes suffering into purifying fire so that all the beings in these worlds can rise to higher forms of existence.[12]*

The Mahāyāna Doctrines in Summary:

❀ Truth is immortal, eternal; it is our *realization* of it that must grow. Here this Principle is *dynamic*, founded on a basis of growth and evolution.

❀ No limitations of time, place, personality, or circumstance can touch the Buddha Principle,

* See also Chap. 3 of this book, "The Tibetan Vajrayāna," p. 83 et seq., and specifically pp. 119-120.

or Essence of Enlightenment. It transcends
them all.

❀ All sentient beings possess the Essence of Buddhahood *now*. One has only to understand this
fact, and then progress in Awareness toward
its realization.

❀ The Mahāyāna provides many means, or "rafts,"
to carry us toward the Other Shore of Enlightenment—meditation "whereby the part
may rebecome the whole"[10] being the greatest
of these. But above and beyond this, deepest
meditation, particularly on the Heart Sūtra
and its Mantra, can lead awareness to THAT
which transcends *all* "shores"—to that Final,
Perfect Enlightenment for which no name can
ever be truly given.

❀ ". . . the Mahāyāna insists on the interdependence and even identity of all life; . . ."[9] Therefore Karma is not individual only, but familial,
national, racial, and universal as well. Thus
all dualistic and egoistic thinking is abolished
here.

❀ Mystical imagery is at the heart of the Mahāyāna
teachings, and Śūnyatā at its root. Events are
looked upon, not in the historical sense, but as
unfolding in the heart and mind of man—

hence the deeply psychological nature of the doctrine. All life is a manifestation of the Buddha Principle, or Mind. Our existence, therefore, is a flux, a process of becoming, and our experience is not outside of ourselves but within; the "self" is not a static thing, but the *Process* as it continually unfolds. Energy is akin to Consciousness, and Consciousness (Mind) is all that *is*.

❀ Salvation (*Nirvāṇa*) is found *within Samsāra*, not by escaping from it. When we try to escape from life, we are assuming that there is a separate self *to* escape. When this is intuitively understood we can live life in the world to the full, with love for all sentient beings who are at-one with us—from the humblest stone to man himself. "This life is a dream, but not one without meaning."[9]

❀ The Mahāyāna, through Nāgārjuna and the Mādhyamika philosophy, has brought the Middle Path doctrine to its apogee. As Humphreys has said: "The Mahāyāna holds a middle position regarding the nature of the world. It is neither real nor unreal. It affirms that it actually exists, but denies its *absolute* reality [italics mine]. Waves exist, but not absolutely."[10] This is the Middle Way between "the Opposites"—between Relative Truth and Absolute Truth.

🏵 At the *highest* level, the Mahāyāna sees *Saṃsāra* and *Nirvāṇa* as *identical*, with Infinite Spirit, Mind, transcending them both. Here again all duality is abolished.

🏵 The older teachings emphasize the "head"— Knowledge; the Mahāyāna emphasizes the "heart"—Compassion. But as in the physical body head and heart both have their necessary place and are integral, functioning parts of the whole, here again the unity of all Buddhism is understood.

These are the basic concepts of the Mahāyāna as I see them.

In conclusion, we return to the final pages of Mahāyāna history.

Buddhism as a whole declined in India during the 11th to 15th centuries due to the resurgence of Brahmanism, invasion of the Moslems, and other causes. Only recently has there been a revival of Buddhism in the land of its origin. This decline led to its spreading outward, the Mahāyāna to the North and East, and the Theravāda to the countries of

Southeast Asia where it had already been deeply established in Ceylon for many centuries, going back to the time of King Aśoka and his son, Mahinda, and daughter, Sanghamitta, who had carried the Buddha's teaching to that beautiful land. Everywhere Buddhism, in whatever form, made spiritual and historical contributions to the life and arts of Asia.

During the 16th to 20th centuries, the dissemination of Western ideas and technology caused adaptations to modern conditions, especially, in the beginning, among those Northern nations such as Japan, where contact with other civilizations and peoples was most strongly felt.

In modern times, continuing the tradition, another great Council, or Conference was held in Rangoon, Burma, in 1954-1956, and following that, still another in Thailand in 1965. Open-minded discussion aimed at the harmonization of differences was the principal theme of the latter Conference. The results led to increased ecumenism, further exchange of literature, reorganization and modernization of schools, and an enhanced growth of social consciousness.

The most recent Conference, in 1969, took place in Kuala Lampur and Penang, and was hosted by the Malaysian Buddhist Fraternity. Here the emphasis was on youth, one youth leader from each Regional

Center taking part. It is axiomatic that in our *youth* lies the future of the world.

Thus ends this brief summary of the history, doctrines, and significance of the Mahāyāna as an integral part of Buddhism. But here, in this concluding paragraph I need not confine myself to one Branch entirely. *All* of Buddhism is moving forward with new impetus as a great world religion and Way of Life which will play no minor part in the world, for it holds the key to a solution of urgent problems which plague us all today. One must search, both outwardly and inwardly, for the meaning of this Key, and use it to the best of one's abilities to unlock the secrets of Ultimate Truth and act upon them. If this is done, a better era should dawn for the world, and the *Kali Yuga,* or dark age, of which the Buddha himself spoke, come to an end in a new Golden Age of Unity for all mankind.

The two following Sections, "Destiny" and "Reincarnation," which complete this Chapter, amplify two specific aspects of the Teaching that have been touched on briefly in preceding pages. Their importance lies in their relevance and immediacy as Buddhism's solutions to enigmas and problems that trouble men's minds today and have done so since the beginning of time. The doctrines discussed are intrinsic to all of Buddhism as I know it.

"DESTINY"[13]

The concept of Destiny, or Fate, as understood in Buddhism, differs widely from the generally accepted one, i.e., that Destiny is a power over which helpless man has no control. In Buddhism, "Destiny" is *self-created*, in the form of Karma. Here it is taught, as we have mentioned in Chapter I (see p. 39) that a man's "fate" today is the result, and only the result of what he has done or thought in the past (either in this life or in previous ones); and that his destiny tomorrow will be the result, and only the result of what he thinks and does today. It is written in the *Dhammapada:* "All that we are is the result of what we have thought: it is founded on our thoughts and made up of our thoughts. If a man speak or act with an evil thought, suffering follows him as a wheel follows the hoof of the beast that draws the cart. . . . If a man speak or act with a good thought, happiness follows him like a shadow that never leaves him." Thus we are the creators of our own destiny—for good or ill, for better or worse. "Every thought [and of course the deed resulting from it] is a Karma," says Upāsaka Ratanasuvanno of Thailand; no power outside of ourselves can impose a "judgment" upon us.

A corollary states (as we have learned before) that it is not the personal self, or "soul," that is carried on under the Law of Karma into other lives, but the consciousness-principle (and in the more highly developed, sometimes even the memories associated with it) that continues to incarnate in other vehicles until Ultimate Enlightenment is achieved. This is the doctrine of *individual* Karma common to both the Southern (Theravāda) and the Northern (Mahāyāna) Schools. In the Mahāyāna, however, the universal aspect of Karma is even more importantly emphasized, that is, Karma as not only collective in a general sense, but specifically as group or family, as national (who has not heard of "the rise and fall of empires" and the causes thereof?), as racial, worldwide, and above all, as *Cosmic*—a framework in which so-called "individual Karma" has an even wider involvement and implication than when taken by itself alone. Dr. D. T. Suzuki has said: "[The spiritual universe] is so closely knitted together that when any part of it or any unit composing it is affected in any way . . . all other parts or units . . . share in the common fate. This subtle spiritual system . . . is like a vast ocean. . . . Even a faint wavelet is sure to spread . . . over its entire surface. . . . Individual Karma, therefore, is not really individual, it is most intimately connected with the whole."[14] This subject will be discussed further in connection with our comment on the Bodhisattva's Vow.

Buddhism also teaches that Karmic destiny is not immutable—it can be overcome, changed, negated— for if such were not the case, we all would be caught in the endless round of *Saṃsāra* (the world of relativity and illusion), from which there would be no deliverance or escape. In the realm of "Thought Karma," causes of whatever nature are stored in the Unconscious (in Buddhist psychology, the *Ālayavi-jñāna,* or Store-Consciousness), and are cumulative in effect unless counteracted by other causes. But right knowledge, character, and *the will to strive for spiritual growth* will free us, and lead to that Liberation for which we strive.

There is also mitigation in the doctrine of *Parināmanā,* or *Parivarta* (the "transferrence of merit" acquired by good and compassionate thoughts and deeds, to another being, or to all beings)—appearing in the Theravāda but developed fully in the Mahāyāna—through deliverance by the Compassion of the Buddhas and Bodhisattvas who, in their boundless love and selfless concern for the welfare of all sentient beings, can save man from *Avidyā* (spiritual ignorance)* and so from the endless round of birth and death and its attendant sorrows. This is not "atonement" as commonly understood—it is more than vicarious sacrifice;† nor is it dependent upon one unique historical event; nor is it arbitrary intervention, as of some "god" or "savior" separate from ourselves to whom we pray in supplication; but it is by means of the guidance and inspiration received *as we open our hearts and minds to the Spiritual Presences around us and within us* (regardless of the names by which we call them), that selfish, ego-instigated desires rooted in ignorance, are destroyed. This "transferrence of merit" by the power of Compassion works inwardly as well as outwardly for those who turn to spiritual sources in their search for Liberation and, most importantly, even for those who are still unawakened to the power and immanent presence of these Sources.

In the Mahāyāna, the Bodhisattva's Vow not to

* See pp. 37-38, 57-59.
† See p. 35.

enter *Nirvāṇa* himself until all sentient beings have
been saved, is not impossible of fulfillment because
here, as mentioned above, Karma is seen as Cosmic.
Everything that exists in the immutable system of
the universe is, in Ultimate Reality, a reflex, or
manifestation of the *Dharmakāya* (the "Body of the
Law," or of Truth—"The *Essence* Body, 'Consciousness merged in Universal Consciousness,'" according
to Humphreys' definition),[6]* that is, of Infinite Mind,
the ocean of Cosmic Being, for which in reality there
can be no limiting name. Therefore it is in Mind, in
Spiritual Consciousness, that all sentient beings are
saved. It is through the application of this Realization, both outwardly in deed and inwardly in
thought, that the Bodhisattvas can bring their saving
"Grace" into visible manifestation.

On one level we turn to the Buddhas and Bodhisattvas for help in overcoming our ignorance and
delusion as to the ultimate reality of material
thoughts and things; on a higher level we realize
that the Buddhas and Bodhisattvas *themselves* are
manifestations of Ultimate Reality and so dwell, not
apart from us in distant heavens, but in that Universal Consciousness of which every sentient being is

* See also p. 56.

a part—and thus, equally, within our own minds and hearts. Whether we turn for help to a realm transcendent to ours (as in *Pūjā* before our shrines) or look within to our immanent Buddha-nature (as in contemplative meditation), we are still working out our own salvation with diligence. And to the degree that we, as potential Buddhas, practice the Bodhisattva's Vow ourselves, to that degree we too are demonstrating our own Bodhisattvahood, and creating a higher "destiny" for all to whom we have dedicated our merits and upon whom our compassion rests.

So no one, or group—national, racial or worldwide, individually or collectively—need be the slave of "Destiny." It is not a mechanical, rigid, or irreversible thing, and the hopeless round of birth and death in *Saṃsāra* need not continue forever. Each one has in his hands and heart the means to Enlightenment—the means to shape his *own* destiny—and has the power within himself to work out his own salvation and to help, and save, others as the Buddha taught. No medicine will cure a sickness unless it is taken, and no means will function unless it is used. Therefore it is up to each one to practice his highest concept of good to the best of his ability, and through his work, thought, and example—growing in grace with the use he makes of them—help to enlighten his own life and through it and the merit he creates and dedicates to others, that of his community, his nation, and the world itself. "Thoughts are things," and wield a power undreamed of by most of us. Wisdom and Compassion are inseparable —in essence *one*—and the exercise of one will bring the other to fruition and lead to that Realization of Truth which lies dormant, like a seed in the heart, waiting patiently as our eternal heritage. Destiny has no power over such as this, nor over those who have found it and are on the Path toward Ultimate Enlightenment.

REINCARNATION[15]

What is "reincarnation"—and who or what is reincarnated?

Dear to the heart of modern man, and of Western man in particular, is the cult of the *individual*—the discrete, self-contained entity who struggles his way through life seeking to overcome not only the obstacles in his own career, but the forces of nature as well—looking outward for "fresh fields to conquer," seldom inward save toward a vaguely envisioned "soul" which he has been taught to believe he is, or has—hoping for eternal rewards in heaven if he is "good," or fearing eternal punishments in hell if he is not. To him, this one life is the sum of his human existence; "evolution" he relegates to the phenomenal worlds; "eternity" has little meaning for him save in terms of a "final judgment" and his own personal fate.

How very circumscribed is this view—how lacking in opportunity for the acquisition of knowledge, for continued growth, for development of inner potentialities and the unfolding of Wisdom, for realization of the essential spiritual nature of man and his unity with all life, and for Enlightenment itself! Growth, in the full evolutionary sense, cannot be accomplished in a day—and "a day" is all that the limited span of one short earth-life can represent on the cosmic scale of eternity. Enmeshed in this belief, what answer can there be to the physical, mental, and environmental inequalities that confront children new-born into the world? How account for their different paths and ends, except to say that "blind fate" or some arbitrary Power outside of themselves has capriciously thrust them, willy-nilly, into a world not of their own making? Would a human parent knowingly afflict his children with such a burden?

How much less would the wise and immutable Law of Life decree such punishments to its many manifestations?

But there is another and very different view, and one that has had a long history even in many of the philosophies of the West—that of *Reincarnation*, or successive rebirths to allow for spiritual evolution through man's own efforts over a sufficient length of time. This view can be divided into two main schools of thought; let us consider each one carefully.

According to the first, "reincarnation" means the successive rebirths of an ego-soul, monad, or entity, inhabiting a new body each round, and carrying forward a process of individual evolution (or sometimes retrogression) depending upon the thoughts and consequent actions that dominate it in each succeeding life, until eventually it returns, disciplined and enlightened, to the Source from whence it came. The controlling force here (as in other views as well) is *Karma*, the Law of Cause and Effect,* which governs the "fate" of each individual according to the uses he makes of his privileges as a thinking entity with free will to follow either "good" or "evil" paths.

This doctrine of an enduring, personal self or

* See the preceding Section on "Destiny," p. 66ff.

soul—passing from life to life no matter how variously "clothed"—appeals to those who still cling to an ego—however rarefied—who still cling, however unwittingly, to the "little self," and cannot yet envision a higher "SELF" in which each realizes his true identity with Universal Consciousness and ceases to differentiate between me and thee, this and that, knower and known, and all the dualities and dichotomies that seem so real on the relative plane of ordinary human thought. This doctrine of a discrete, reincarnating entity contains its own contradiction, for how can unity with the Divine Source, the Absolute, ever be realized while belief in a separate self remains?

According to the second view, "reincarnation" (as we have discussed in other contexts in Chapter I)* signifies a carrying forward under the Law of Karma, not of an illusory, personal ego-soul, but of the life-force, or stream of consciousness, built up in each succeeding life on all that has gone before, and in turn creating the Karmic forces which will affect the course of its future evolution. They deny the doctrine of an enduring "self"—which to them is as perishable and transient as the body it is presumed to inhabit. Again we are reminded of the illustration

* See pp. 6, 39-41.

of the candle and the flame, mentioned on page 41.

No one, however, disputes the fact that Karma underlies the reincarnation process. Breaking free from this Birth-and-Death cycle—the attainment of *Nirvāṇa*—can only be accomplished by the will to seek and unfold one's own Enlightenment, the effort to uncover that Reality which lies latent, buried in most of us under layers of spiritual ignorance and delusion as to our real nature and the meaning and purpose of life.

Which of these two schools of thought provides the most logical answer to the reincarnation problem?

While one must reason from the standpoint of his own understanding at any given time and level, I do not believe that merely doctrinal questions, or even semantics, are of primary importance here—for the basic realizations gained over many thousands of years by the seers and saints of all the world's great religions are in essence the same. Let us consider some of them, and continue with the question: *What* is it that reincarnates?

It is evident that all the component elements of the reincarnation process are in a continual state of flux, or *becoming*—nothing is static or "fixed"—and that the moving force behind it all must be a *mental*

76

one—not on the relative and human, but on the Cosmic and spiritual scale. Let us call it MIND for want of a better term, for we must use words and concepts in the course of a discussion, although these are only stepping-stones—"intellectual approximations," as someone has said, "to what in the end must be realized intuitively."

It is obvious that the physical body and its senses, which dissolve at death, cannot reincarnate. Then what of this "I" in which most of us take such great store? Let us, for the sake of argument, call its elements "The Five Skandhas," or "The Five Aggregates," as the Buddha did. These were discussed in another context earlier in this book,* but it might be well to review them now. They consist of:

- the physical body and its senses—already considered and dismissed;
- feelings and sensations (dependent upon the body and its senses);
- emotional reactions or volition (dependent upon feelings and sensations);
- perceptions leading to memory (dependent upon all that preceded them); and
- consciousness.

* See p. 40.

Take all these away at death, and what have you left? Certainly nothing that can be called a "self" remains. Nāgasena, in *The Questions of King Milinda* (Gr.: Menander) compared them to the parts of a chariot (wheels, body, shafts, etc.). Only when they are functioning *together* do we have something called a "chariot." Scattered, the "chariot" ceases to exist.

But is there something more?

In the living being a constant interaction is taking place between the Five Skandhas—and "action" and "reaction" is the heart of Karma. What is it that *animates* this stream of consciousness, this character and, for that matter, the force of Karma itself? Let us go back to the term we first used—Mind, Consciousness—the Source and Ground from which both logic and intuition tell us that all manifestation must arise. Some call it "The Void,"* or "The Plenum Void"—"THAT from which all manifested things emerge and to which all manifested things return." Allied with this, and forming the bridge between them, is the Ālaya, or Store-consciousness† where the memories of man and of all sentient life lie wait-

* See pp. 51-52.
† See pp. 51, 68.

78

ing to be tapped when the time is ripe. Here we find wheels within wheels, symbolized in Buddhism by the Tibetan "Wheel of Life,"* turning purposefully and slowly in the natural course of evolution, turning more rapidly as the enlightened mind and will follow the Path and depart not from it. Thus we can see that Mind alone is unchanging, and the Ground of our being alone, eternal. All life, as an emanation of Mind, partakes of its nature, and so continues in repeatedly manifested forms until Ultimate Enlightenment—*Nirvāna*—frees us from the Wheel of Existence.

Due to the limitations of language we must use the personal pronoun when speaking of "his" or "my" former incarnations, of "his" or "my" future ones; but this is a misnomer. To speak of one *who* reincarnates, if we are not careful in our thinking, draws us back to the stultifying concept of a permanent ego and all its concomitant illusions. But identification with Universal Mind, Spirit, Thatness, or Thusness—the Ground of all being—opens for us an endless vista of Consciousness far beyond anything conceivable by the little self—a Consciousness beyond either good or evil, diversity or unity—

* See pp. 59-60.

inexpressible, and only to be gained through Ultimate Enlightenment itself.

We carry our future in the palms of our hands today; and so there is hope and final certainty of an unending vista of LIFE, of a supernal State of Consciousness whose glimmerings, even now, lighten our inmost hearts as each travels his Path toward the Goal.

NOTE

After writing this Section I had occasion, through correspondence, to encounter a number of people (Buddhists and others) holding differing views on the reincarnation question. Seeking a common ground and an acceptable resolution, I looked more extensively into the records of other controversies, in early Buddhism, leading to certain resolutions arrived at in the developing Mahāyāna. One result of this was the Section on "Origins, Doctrines, and Significance of the Mahāyāna," included in this Chapter (see page 46 ff.). But, more importantly, the resolutions I found were extremely relevant to the present question; and as the lack of unanimity among my correspondents and Buddhist friends is not confined to them alone, I venture to quote in part, and at the risk of some repetition, my findings as they appeared in the November, 1969, issue of *The Middle Way.*

"[Seeking a resolution of opposing views on the reincarnation problem as posed to me], I went back into the early history of Buddhism and the controversies arising from differing interpretations of the Scriptures, notably that between such opposing views on the nature of Reality as those of the Sarvāstivādins (3rd century B.C.), i.e., all that is evident to the physical senses is real, and those of the Mahāsanghikas (1st century A.D.), i.e., nothing that is evident to the physical senses is real.* Nāgārjuna, in the 2nd century, pondering this question, founded the Mādhyamika, or 'Middle Doctrine' School to harmonize conflicting ideas of the nature of Reality by his doctrine of Relative *versus* Absolute Truth, the foundation of both being Śūnyatā, or Voidness. . . .†

"Now why could not a similar harmonization of present contentions be applicable here, employing the principle of Relative *vs.* Absolute Truth as it functions for us at our *present level*? Relatively speaking, *something* (life-force, consciousness-principle) carries on—whether here or elsewhere—perhaps for a long time to come until, through Karma, all problems of a *Saṃsāric* nature are resolved. Here we are still in the realm of *Saṃsāra*, even up to the "Heavens of Form" where the Bodhisattvas "see each other" in the spiritual Body of Bliss, the *Sambhogakāya*. Beyond this (inconceivable in direct terms to the mundane mind) lies the Dharmakāya, immanent as the impersonal Ground of Buddhahood—the Buddha-nature inherent in every being.

"In our present state, however, few indeed can *realize* this Truth and reach this Goal at *one bound*. Rebirth

* See p. 50.
† See p. 51.

(reincarnation), wherever and in whatever form, is a means for this unfoldment—a means to an end, but *never the end in itself*. In this view, 'rebirth' is not inconsistent with the ultimate goal, which puts an end to all rebirth and is *Nirvāṇa* itself.

"To my mind there is no conflict here because (as our minds conceive of these matters) they are on *different levels,* i.e., the Relative and the Absolute. But since, in the final analysis as set forth in the Mahāyāna, *Saṃsāra* and *Nirvāṇa* are *identical,** all we have been discussing resolves itself into *One*, and in a realization of this One, we are led to that ineffable Ultimate which *transcends* it. Whether this realization comes through the 'sudden Enlightenment' of Zen, or through the longer, evolutionary path of rebirth, it is herein alone that our ultimate salvation lies."

* See pp. 63, 103.

3

THE TIBETAN VAJRAYĀNA —MARPA AND MILAREPA, AND THE KARGYUDPA SCHOOL[16]

INTRODUCTION

The Tantric Vajrayāna of Buddhist Tibet has been a controversial subject for years, in both East and West. Part of this is due to varied, often fundamental misunderstandings, part due to malpractices and degradations perpetrated upon it in the past by a few ignorant, perverted, and misguided "practitioners." The very climate of Tibet, with its high and lonely snow-mountains, its rarefied air, its profound silences, leads to introverted tendencies which, in the human mind, can result in either the highest spiritual development or in the lowest of misdirected aims. Old Tibet was a mixture of both, "and of much that lies between."[10] The following material may help to explain these anomalies, and bring to light all that has been, and is, of highest value and highest good in Tibetan Tantric Buddhism as it emerged, through all vicissitudes, in that once mysterious "Land of the Snows."

Buddhism as a whole has always maintained, as we know, the most tolerant attitude of all religions toward different faiths and peoples, absorbing elements from the various cultures into which it has moved without changing its fundamental character, and in this case the elements surrounding it when it first entered Tibet were strangely alien to those known in the more southerly Buddhist world. Tantric influences from India, with their sexual symbology as expressed in paintings and images, arrived in Tibet with Padma Sambhava in the 8th century, and the native religion, the Bön—shamanistic and filled with strange psychic practices and superstitions—could not fail in the early days to exert its influence, since it was bitterly opposed to the incursion of the higher faith.

In Tantrism, sexual symbolism has always played a prominent role—expressive of the spiritual ecstasy of union with the Ineffable Source (as such symbolism has always appeared, from time immemorial, in all religions. On the *human* level, the loss of "oneself" in the unity of love with another is the deepest and most powerful psychic and emotional experience known to man—a prototype of that ineffable *spiritual* experience of union with the Divine* for which every devotee yearns).

But under the circumstances prevalent in Tibet and elsewhere at the time, these ideals were peculiarly open to misinterpretation. There were dangers, and the human mind is a difficult thing to control, though warnings were never absent.

It was not until the reform movements set in, beginning in the 11th century with the famous Indian Mahāyāna monk, Atisha, who founded the Kahdampa Order, followed by Marpa and Milarepa, founders of the Kargyudpa School, and carried on by Tsongkhapa in the 15th century, that the Buddhist Tantric Vajrayāna strongly reasserted its fundamental spiritual character and condemned all practices not based upon the exalted ideals of its founders.

This chapter will emphasize the basic teachings and practice of the Kargyudpa School, with which the author is most familiar, without neglecting the history and background from whence they came. This School is not untypical of all the movements

---

* See pp. 35, 92 for a Buddhist definition of "Divine."

which followed it—esoteric only in the sense that the highest teachings were never written down, but were passed on orally from Guru to disciple. No "exclusiveness" was implied here—only that a student or disciple must be *prepared*, before the higher teachings could be revealed to him by his Guru— step by step as he proved himself worthy to receive them. Without experience, and deep, intuitive understanding gained through *practice*, the higher teachings leading to Ultimate Enlightenment could have been wasted or ignorantly misused; and preservation and transmissal in their purest form was the dedicated aim of all the great Masters and Teachers of Tibet.

MILAREPA

The life and times of Milarepa, the great Tibetan Buddhist Poet-Saint of the 11th to 12th century, and the teachings of the School which he and his Guru Marpa founded, are subjects that could occupy many volumes.[17] To cover them at all adequately in one short chapter will result in little more than a sketch; but I shall fill in as many of the outlines as I can. Above all, I shall try to bring you some small glimpse of the extraordinary panorama of Milarepa's dedi-

cated life and the exuberance and joy in the Dharma
that were his. His life was a complete devotion to
and immersion in the Buddha-Truth.

Milarepa was second in the line of transmission
Gurus of the Kargyudpa, or Mahāmudrā School of
the Tibetan Vajrayāna. This School has maintained
its Succession unbroken down to the present day.

Milarepa's life spanned more than 80 years, at a
time when Islam and its culture were spreading
throughout all Hindustan. It is owing to him, and to
his Guru, Marpa the Translator, that much of
Buddhism's spiritual heritage, then threatened with
destruction, was preserved.

There has been no teacher in the history of Tibet
to surpass Milarepa for the depth, breadth, and
transcendency of his vision or for the place he held
and still holds in the minds and hearts of his people.
He had a fine singing voice, and the classic "Hundred Thousand Songs" (this figure symbolizing an
unknown, but very large number) is familiar to all
Tibetans. Herdsmen still sang many of them in the
high pastures of the Himālayas until the Chinese
Communists silenced them. The block-printed
"Songs"[18] (with the 61 stories that frame them)—
recently translated into English in their entirety by
a modern disciple, Garma C.C. Chang (the Chang
Chen-chi of *The Practice of Zen*) and embodying

the whole gamut of Buddhist teachings, Theravāda, Mahāyāna, and Vajrayāna—were born of Milarepa's genius and Enlightenment, and of the silences and spiritual grandeur of the great Snow Mountains where he dwelt in caves, taught the people, and meditated on the Illuminating Void. They carry a message as pertinent today as it was when he sang and preached them ("in a tuneful voice like that of the God Brahmā," so the records say) to humble villagers and disciples; to Yogis, Pandits, and scholars; to demons and magic beings; and even to the animals, in the High Himālayas so many centuries ago.

Milarepa has been compared to Saint Francis of Assisi, strange as this comparison might seem to both of them, for his love for and devotion to all sentient beings, for simple living and high endeavor, for his unwavering adherence to Truth as it was revealed to him, and for his place in the hearts and minds of his people.

HISTORY

To go back somewhat in time, the early history of the arrival in Tibet of the mystical Vajrayāna (the

"Thunderbolt," or "Adamantine Path" form of Tantric Buddhism later adopted by the Kargyudpa School of Marpa and Milarepa) is an extremely interesting one. Buddhism had been known in Tibet to a certain degree, it is believed, for some 200 years prior to the reign, in the middle of the 7th century A.D., of Tibet's great King, Srong-btsan-Gam-po— the first Tibetan ruler to unify the country politically. He may have been a Buddhist prior to his marriages, but the best-known story credits his conversion to his two Buddhist wives—one, the Nepalese Princess Brikhuti, and the other, a daughter of the Chinese Imperial House (the T'ang) by the name of Wen-cheng—whom he married in A.D. 641. The two princesses brought many Buddhist objects with them to Tibet, and were later canonized as the Green and White aspects, respectively, of the Divine Mother Tārā (or Dölma) the Merciful—"She who with compassion guides travelers across the ocean of transmigration."

We learn of Srong-btsan's dispatch of the scholar-emissary, Thorna-Sambhoti (Sambhota) to India to collect Buddhist scriptures for translation into Tibetan, thus beginning the process of saving for posterity much that was later lost in the land of its origin; of Sambhota's formulation of a Tibetan alphabet modeled on the beautiful Sanskrit Devanāgarī characters (said to be of divine origin) then in use in Kashmir; and of Sambhota's construction of Tibet's first systematic, written grammar.

The founding of the Kargyudpa School's principal predecessor, the Ñingmapa, or "Red Hats," in A.D. 749-755 by Padma Sambhava under the patronage of King Tisong-Detsen, followed; and Samyé, Tibet's first monastery, was founded in A.D. 779. It was Padma Sambhava, as we have mentioned, who brought the earliest forms of Buddhist Tantra to Tibet. The establishment of the *last* great School, the Gelugpa, or "Yellow Hats," the "Reformed" School of Tsongkhapa to which the Dalai Lama and Panchen Lama belong, took place at the beginning of the 15th century.

Between these two, in the 11th century A.D., the Kargyudpa School of Marpa and Milarepa had its beginnings. As a semi-reformed sect, this School retained the Tantric knowledge and practice, but purified them of all corruptions which had seeped in during the previous 200 years because of the aforementioned Bön (indigenous, shamanistic) influences and a breaking down of monastic discipline, adhering only to their original spiritual and esoteric

90

meanings. Monastic discipline was reaffirmed, and celibacy enjoined upon all monks.

Both India to the South and China on Tibet's eastern borders were highly civilized during these times, when Europe was still in a comparatively barbaric age. As early as the 7th century, culture was flowing into Tibet from its neighbors to the East and South. At the time of Milarepa (1052-1135) the culture of Tibet had risen to a high level, comparable to that of the Western world of the same period and surpassing it in philosophical and religious development.

The Kargyudpa Succession traces its origin to the Indian Pandit Tilopa (believed to have been an incarnation of Amitābha, the Buddha of Life and Light), who flourished in the 10th century, and to his disciple, Nāropā, Professor of Philosophy at the celebrated Indian Buddhist University of Nālanda, who was Marpa's principal Guru. According to tradition, Tilopa received the Mahāmudrā Teaching* by revelation from Dorje-Chang (Skt.: Vajradhāra), the Divine Buddha—analogous to the Ādi, or Celestial Buddha of the Ñingmapa School, and venerated

* See pp. 105, 108-109, 112-113, for a discussion of Mahāmudrā.

by the Gelugpas as an emanation of Buddha Śākya-muni. In no way, however, should the Ādibuddha be regarded as a God-Creator—a theistic concept totally foreign to Buddhist teachings. To super-impose a form of monotheism on the Buddhist ethic, as asserted by some scholars, is completely errone-ous, and has no place in the Buddhist Tantras or in Buddhism generally. As Govinda has written: "The word 'divine' . . . is not to be understood in a theistic sense, but as 'exalted,' as going beyond the range of human sense-perception, belonging to the highest spiritual experience."[11] And again: "The Ādibuddha is the symbol of the universality, timelessness, and completeness of the enlightened mind . . . the passive aspect of pure *Tathatā*, or Suchness . . . the potential Buddhahood inherent in every being."[11] That Bud-dhism is nontheistic in the Western sense is an important point to remember, for neither the Kargy-udpa School, nor the Mahāyāna generally, as we have said before, deifies either the Buddha himself or any aspect of the Buddha-Mind.

The "Tantric Pantheon," as represented in the iconography of Tibet, merely symbolizes, or personi-fies in sculptured or graphic form, different aspects of this Principle, such as Perfect Wisdom, Perfect Com-passion, Perfect Knowledge and the like, or (as in the case of the so-called "Wrathful Deities"), fierce strength and courage in the struggle against ignorance and delusion. As *Cosmic forces* operating in man "which all great beings, high and low, to some extent enshrine,"[10] they are not of a concrete but of *a mental and psychological nature*, and are never regarded by the high Lamas as discrete entities or "gods" separate from man or from his inner consciousness.*

Tilopa, in turn, handed on the teaching orally, as an esoteric doctrine—hence the appellation "Whispered Succession"—to Nāropā, who in turn transmitted it to Marpa, and Marpa to Milarepa. In one of his Songs, Milarepa says of himself:

> Great Dorje-Chang is my origin,
> Wise good Tilo my ancestor,
> Great Pandit Nāro my Grandfather,
> Marpa the Translator my honored Father.[18]

The monk-physician Gambopa, Milarepa's disciple and successor (1079-1161), followed in the line of Transmission Gurus. Gambopa organized the School on a firm basis as a blending of theoretical exposition as found in the Sūtras, with the experimental and experiential practices of the Buddhist Tantras.[19]

* See also pp. 99-101, 119.

In conclusion, the time of Marpa and Milarepa was also that of Buston, the great Tibetan historian and writer, who first classified the *Kanjur*, or "The Translation of the Word"—the first part of the Tibetan Buddhist Canon, consisting of 108 volumes, and concerned with discipline, philosophy, doctrines, and the virtues of the Bodhisattvas. The *Kanjur* as classified by Buston contained elements of all three great Branches of Buddhism—Theravāda, Mahā-yāna, and Vajrayāna—an attitude unequivocally subscribed to by Milarepa and by the Kargyudpa School. Most of the *Kanjur* is a careful translation from the Sanskrit and Chinese, of inestimable value where the original material has been lost. The *Tanjur*, the second part of the Canon, is a collection of 225 volumes of works by Indian Buddhist masters—commentaries on the Sūtras and Tantras, but irrelevant to our present discussion.

LIFE

The accounts of Milarepa's life are mainly derived from the *Namthar*, or *Mila Kahbum—The Life of Milarepa*—which has been so ably translated into English by the Tibetan scholar, Lama Kazi Dawa-

94

Samdup, and edited by Dr. W. Y. Evans-Wentz under the title: *Tibet's Great Yogi, Milarepa.*[17] This biography is thought by many to have been written by Milarepa's disciple, Rachungpa (who occupies a prominent place in the narratives introducing and surrounding the Songs). But according to Professor Guenther, the "Life" was actually written by the famous and mysterious Yogi, gTsan.sMyon.Heruka —"The Mad Yogi from Tsan"—a pupil of Gambopa.[19] Professor Guenther's findings are quoted by Mr. Chang in an Appendix to the "Songs," and the following biographical sketch is based in part on Mr. Chang's account in this same book.[20]

Milarepa was born in Guṅthaṅ, Tibet, A.D. 1052, living in approximately the same period as the Christian monks, Robert and Bruno, founders of the Carthusian and Cistercian Orders, respectively.

Milarepa's early life was full of sorrow and misfortune. While still a boy, upon the untimely death of his wealthy father, he, his mother and sister, were cheated of their inheritance by greedy and unscrupulous relatives, who forced them to live in abject poverty as family servants. Finally, after many years of hard labor and humiliation, life had become so unendurable that Milarepa was persuaded by his mother to seek redress by magic, since there seemed to be no other way. At her instigation, therefore, he sought out a famous sorcerer, and soon mastered a method for producing violent hail storms. He then unloosed such a storm upon his relatives, destroying their crops and houses and bringing death to many of them.

Afterward, appalled by his sin and filled with remorse, he vowed to atone by a life of complete dedication to the Dharma. In pursuit of this objective he studied under a number of teachers and Gurus, even receiving initiation into the profound teaching of "The Great Perfection"* of the Ñingmapa School, but "the shadows of sin and pride" continued to defeat him. Finally, at the suggestion of one of his teachers, he sought out the great Guru Marpa, who had recently returned to Tibet from India "after many years of study and practice there."

Forewarned in a dream, Marpa recognized Milarepa as a destined disciple who would one day become the greatest teacher of Tibet. Keenly aware, however, that he was still in need of much chastening and discipline, Marpa subjected him for eight long years to severe trials and hardships, among them the building and tearing down of one stone

* (The Ñingmapa form of) the *Mahāmudrā* teaching which will be discussed later (see pp. 105, 108-109, 112-113).

house after another on a desolate mountainside. Symbolically, this undoubtedly represents the repeated struggles toward self-mastery and the repeated failures of a still faulty and immature disciple. Milarepa comments on the lessons learned from this experience as follows:

> Faith is the firm foundation of my house,
> Diligence forms the high walls,
> Meditation makes the huge stones,
> And Wisdom is the great cornerstone.
> With these four things I built my castle,
> And it will last as long as the Truth eternal.[21]

At last, having overcome all hindrances, Milarepa was rewarded, accepted by Marpa as a fully qualified disciple, and initiated as his spiritual son.

Eleven months of solitary meditation in a mountain cave followed, leading to "direct Realization and an initial achievement on the Path of Bodhi." Thus began Milarepa's spiritual career. From then on he studied the Scriptures of all Buddhist Schools, both Southern and Northern (for the Kargyudpa values the teachings of *all* Schools), and meditated with constancy and devotion.

Now, having dreamed of his mother's death, he left Marpa and returned to his home, to find his dream confirmed—the land desolate, his house in ruins, and his mother's bones lying amid the fallen stones. His sister had vanished, he knew not where. Vividly confronted with the pain of fleeting human existence, "an anguish of desire to renounce the world" overcame him, and he solemnly vowed to meditate in the remote mountains without interruption until he had reached the Ultimate Enlightenment. This vow he kept, dwelling alone in a cave for 12 years and subsisting "on nothing but nettles until his body became greenish in hue." Finally, strengthened by a vision of Marpa (about which he sings in one of the most poignant of his Songs) he reached his Goal—attaining freedom and miraculous powers.

After this his fame spread far and wide. His life of wandering across the borderlines of Tibet and Nepal then began. He attracted many disciples—Pandits, monks, Yogis, and lay followers, both men and women—teaching all through his inspired words and songs, and initiating those who, after trial, proved worthy to become his spiritual sons and daughters.

Milarepa died at Čhubar in 1135, at the age of 83, and his body was cremated there. Legend recounts that his earthly remains were carried away by the "Sky-Travelers," the *Ḍākinīs*, or fairy beings, whom he had converted and befriended throughout his ministry on earth. In his later years Milarepa was given the title "Jetsun," or "Holy Mila," by all Tibetans, and is regarded today as "the greatest poet, Yogi, and Saint in Tibetan history."[29]

The Ḍākinīs

Before turning to the Doctrines, I would like to say a further word about the *Ḍākinīs* (or *Khadomas* as they are called in Tibet), as they play a prominent role in Milarepa's songs and experiences.

Exoterically, these "Sky-Travelers" are presented as ethereal beings or "goddesses" belonging to various orders, both worldly and spiritual. Noted for their magical powers, they may assume many forms —divine or human, peaceful or demonical and terrifying, beautiful or strange—like the "five pigeons" in one of Milarepa's storied encounters with them.

Esoterically, however, their reality lies in the inner experience of meditation—a reality far greater, from the Buddhist point of view, "than that of the so-called material objects, because it . . . springs directly from spiritual awareness and not from the roundabout way of the peripheral senses. . . . [The *Ḍākinī,* therefore] appears to the earnest seeker, especially to the practicing Yogi . . . to lead him on the way of higher knowledge and conscious realization."[11]

The word *Khadoma,* meaning space or ether, is metaphysically equivalent to *Śūnyatā,* the Great Void. Hence the *Ḍākinīs* symbolize powerful forces of a Cosmic nature *manifesting in the human mind during meditation*—as, in one form or another, do all the personifications found in the Tantric pantheon (see pp. 92-93). In the Buddhist *Maṇḍalas** the *Ḍākinīs* appear as the female, or passive, counterparts (representing *Prajñā,* Perfect Wisdom) of the *Dhyāni* Buddhas and Bodhisattvas†—who, themselves, personify the active force of *Karunā,* or Perfect Compassion. Metaphysically, Wisdom and Compassion are a *unity.* The Divine Mother *Tārā,*

---

* *Maṇḍalas* are ritual circles or diagrams used in Tibetan Buddhist initiations and meditation practice as metaphysical and esoteric representations of the Universe, i.e., the *outer* Cosmos (the macrocosm) and the *inner* Cosmos (the microcosm) within the meditator, which are realized as an essential Unity.

† The five *Dhyāni,* or Meditation Buddhas depicted, with their Wisdom qualities, in Tibetan *Maṇḍalas.* They personify aspects of the Ādi, or primordial Buddha (see pp. 91-92)—the Total Unity as seen in meditation, and occupy the center and the four quarters of the *Maṇḍala.* By identification with the *Center,* the Totality from which the Cosmos is generated, man finds the macrocosm within the microcosm—which is himself.[22]

or "the faithful Dölma" as she is known in Tibet, is one of these *Khadomas*, a Bodhisattva in her own right who, as Tibet's Patron Goddess, is especially revered because "she represents the very essence of [Madonna-like], loving devotion . . . [extending] her loving care to the good and the bad, the wise and the foolish, like the sun that shines for sinners as well as for saints."[11] In the beautiful language of the Scriptures, Tārā was born from one of Avalokiteś-vara's tears. Exoterically or esoterically, the fusion of Wisdom and Compassion in Tārā is one of the most potent and beautiful aspects of Tibetan Buddhism.

DOCTRINES

A full discussion of the Tantric Vajrayāna and the doctrines of the Kargyudpa School, even were it possible, could be endless, beyond the scope of any one book, and certainly beyond the powers of this author. Those who are interested in further research may find enlightening material in the literature, notably in the W. Y. Evans-Wentz *Tibetan Series*.[23] Anagarika Govinda's *Foundations of Tibetan Mysticism*[11] contains a wealth of enlightening material, as does Garma C. C. Chang's *Teachings of Tibetan Yoga*,[24] and his Commentary and Notes in *The Hundred Thousand Songs of Milarepa*.[18] It goes without saying that the "Songs" themselves should be read, for in them, as Mr. Chang has commented: "Milarepa has left us a treasury of valuable information on his personal Yogic experiences, and advice and instructions concerning the practical problems of meditation."

Some of the methods employing visualization of, and identification with the Guru or Patron Buddha, and other visualization techniques—a prominent feature of this system—are described in Edward Conze's *Buddhist Meditation*,[25] by Mircea Eliade in his *Yoga: Immortality and Freedom*,[26] in Mr. Chang's *Teachings of Tibetan Yoga*,[24] in Evans-Wentz,[23] and elsewhere. Here, I can only touch upon a few of the basic premises and methods which underlie the practices as a whole—*all* of which were founded upon "the supreme truth of Śūnyatā, or Voidness— the principle that stresses," again to quote Mr. Chang, "the nonexistence of the 'substance' of all beings—the relative, flowing, and ungraspable nature of all phenomenal things."[18] As we have already learned, this is one of the most important doc-

trines of the Mahāyāna, as well as of Tibetan Tantrism. Here, too, a primary principle of the *Mādhyamika* (Middle Doctrine) of Nāgārjuna will be
recognized, and of the *Prajñāpāramitā* (Perfection
of Wisdom) literature (see pp. 52-53) so basic to the
Zen School; and, as we shall see later, a practical
application of the Mind-Only doctrine of *Yogācāra*
philosophy (referred to on pp. 51-52), as well as
an intimation of the *Hwa Yen* (Jap.: *Kegon*) principle of the mutual interpenetration of all things in
the *Dharmadhātu* (the State of Ultimate Reality,
the unoriginated root of Cosmic Truth).[38] Mādhyamika has often been referred to as " the theory of
Voidness," and Mahāmudrā as "the practice of Voidness." A corollary is that, in Absolute Transcendence
(*Śūnya*, the Void), *Saṃsāra* (the world) and *Nirvāṇa* (the Ultimate Perfection) are *identical*—as
spoken of in previous pages—facets of our own
experience. From the *Absolute* point of view, one
cannot distinguish between the world and *Nirvāṇa*,
for then *Nirvāṇa* would be reduced to one of a pair
of opposites and so would no longer *be Nirvāṇa*,
which is transcendent. To quote Conze:[27] "The doctrine of Emptiness (i.e., the absence of 'things'—that
which goes beyond both the finite and the infinite)
is not taught to support one theory against others,

but to get rid of theories altogether." Finally the Vajrayāna *discipline*, aiming at the conquest of the illusory self, is basic to the Tantric goal of Mahāmudrā.

Mr. Chang comments:[28] "Tibetan Tantrism [Tantric Yoga] is a form of practical Buddhism abounding in methods and techniques for carrying out the practice of all the Mahāyāna teachings.... [It] lays most of its stress on practice [leading to] Realization, rather than on philosophical speculations." In this view, all existence and manifestation is found to be within one's own experience, that is, within one's own mind. Perfect mastership of one's mind leads to Enlightenment, to Buddhahood, for Mind—Universal Intelligence—is its source. All beings, therefore, are Buddhas in essence—unenlightened only to the extent that their Buddha-Mind has not yet been unfolded.

To this end, in Tibetan Tantrism (Mr. Chang continues) "two major approaches are provided for differently disposed individuals: The Path of Means [Energy Yoga] and The Path of Liberation [Mind Yoga]. The former [approach] stresses ... the practice of taming the *Prāṇa* [vital energy]...." This is accomplished through a variety of psychophysical techniques (see p. 106ff.), amply (though never completely), described in the literature (see pp. 101-102). The *latter* method stresses "an approach through taming the *mind*. Both approaches, however, are based on the truism of the identicality of mind and *Prāṇa*, which is the fundamental theorem of Tantrism."[29]

Here we find the same principle of Unity that is reiterated again and again in all the Mahāyāna teachings. Every duality, apparently antithetical (positive and negative, noumenon and phenomenon, vitality and voidness, mind and *Prāṇa*, etc.) is, in fact, an inseparable *unity,* manifesting in different forms. A coin may have two sides, yet it is still one coin.

The obvious conclusion based upon this premise is that "if one's consciousness, or mind is disciplined . . . illuminated, and sublimated, so will be his *Prāṇas* and vice versa. The practice that stresses taming the *Prāṇa* is called 'The Yoga With Form,' or 'The Path of Means' [an exertive practice]. [That which] stresses taming the mind is called 'The Yoga Without Form,' or 'The Path of Liberation' . . . a natural and effortless one known as Mahāmudrā."[29]

These two practices exist as separate Paths only in the early stages, however. In advanced stages they converge and become one. Most of Tibet's great

Yogis practiced *both* in order to hasten their spiritual progress—either simultaneously or by using one to supplement the other, as did Milarepa.

The Yoga With Form

Advanced forms of breathing exercises, combined with *Mantra* (invocation through the power of sound), visualization, and other thought-processes; use of the *Mala,* or "prayer beads"* (which nearly every Tibetan wears or carries); and the *Tumo,* or Heat Yoga practice—in the form developed and systematized by Nāropā—are examples of the Yoga With Form. *Tumo* is the mystic "inner fire" produced in the Navel Center during Buddhist Yoga practice, and is basic to all other practices, because of its deep psychophysical significance as psychic heat associated with the warmth of spiritual emotion and "the fire of spiritual integration."[11] It is also one of the factors that make it possible for Yogis such as Mila to live happily in the bitter cold of the High Himālayas clad only in a single cotton garment. "Repa" *means* cotton-clad, and was the distinguishing mark of Milarepa and his disciples. White cotton cloth, in Tibetan symbology, also is emblematic of the spiritual intellect.

*See author's article on "Buddhist Meditation Beads," p. 244, *The Mountain Path,* October, 1973.

Since *Tumo* holds a unique place in the Tibetan Vajrayāna, it should be differentiated from the perhaps better-known "Serpent Fire," personified by the Goddess *Kuṇḍalinī*, of the Hindu Tantrics. In the latter, the *Śakti*, or *Power Aspect*—the *Kuṇḍalinī*-fire quiescent at the base of the spine—is visualized as a coiled serpent to be awakened by the Yogi and raised to permeate the whole body with its physical, spiritual, and psychic heat, leading to inner power and spiritual freedom. Here, as in *all* advanced Yogic techniques, there are elements of danger. None, in Buddhism or elsewhere, should ever be attempted without the guidance of a Guru or qualified teacher.

In the *Buddhist* system, it is the *Prajñā*, or *Wisdom Aspect* in its intuitive form—at the *Navel* Center and personified by the *Ḍākinī*, or *Khadoma*—which becomes the leading principle and ignites the spiritual flame. The *Śakti Kuṇḍalinī*, while never denied, is not included in the Path of Meditation.

Lack of space here prevents a detailed account of the Yogic system of psychic anatomy, but innumerable descriptions and diagrammatic illustrations may be found in the literature. Suffice it to say that of the seven *Cakras*, or psychic nerve centers situated along the spinal area, only four are emphasized in Buddhist practice, although none of the others are denied.

Govinda says:[11]

> In Buddhist Yoga . . . the disciple is advised [to]
> meditate on the four [upper] *Cakras* (or planes of con-
> sciousness) . . . the Crown and Throat Centers . . . [and]
> the Heart and Navel Centers. . . . Concentration is di-
> rected upon the [three] main Channels, or *Nāḍīs* (*Iḍā,
> Piṅgalā, and Suṣumṇā*), the main power-currents [of the
> body, generally considered to be located in the median
> duct, and on either side of the spinal column—psychic
> counterparts of the physical nervous system—whose grav-
> itational force is modified] through a temporal damming-
> up of the energy content of the upper Centers. . . .
>
> In the deepest sense, therefore, *Tumo* signifies the
> fire of spiritual integration [in Milarepa's Biography
> called "The warming breath of *Khadomas*"] which fuses
> all polarities . . . and kindles the flame of inspiration from
> which is born the power of Renunciation. . . . This pro-
> cess is represented by the Flame, or Flaming Drop [Skt.:
> *Bindu;* Tib.: *Tig Le*].

Milarepa's translator comments:[29] "The statement
that 'the Divinity of Buddhahood is omnipresent,
but the quickest way to realize it is to discover it
within one's own body-mind complex,' will apply to
every technique of Buddhist Tantric Yoga except
Mahāmudrā."

Those who might like to go more deeply into
the roots of this matter will find much of value not

only in Govinda's book, but in Eliade's chapter on "Yoga Techniques in Buddhism,"[26] in Chang's chapter on "Buddha and Meditation,"[30] and of course in Evans-Wentz' "Tibetan Yoga and Secret Doctrines."[23]

So much for the Yoga With Form.

The Yoga Without Form

In the Yoga Without Form, on the other hand, the Path of Liberation—Mahāmudrā, or the Great Symbol—is best expressed in the words of Milarepa himself:

> Buddha cannot be found by searching,
> So contemplate your own MIND.[18]

The translator comments: "This sentence is extremely important as representing the essence of the Mahāmudrā teaching, for Illumination and Voidness are the two immanent characteristics of Mind."[18] It is the Buddha-Mind within that concerns us here.

Mr. Chang continues: "In general Buddhism, one is taught to *search* for Enlightenment and to *attain* Buddhahood; but in Mahāmudrā the Guru points out to the disciple that ONE'S OWN MIND IS BUDDHA HIMSELF, and therefore to *search* for anything, even Buddhahood, is a waste of time." Evans-Wentz, in

The Tibetan Book of the Great Liberation, has said:
"The microcosmic mind [that is, the mind of sentient
beings], being the off-spring of the Macrocosmic
Mind [the Mind of the Universe] may, by the process
of Yoga, attain ecstatic consciousness of its parental
source, and become one with it in essence."[23] In the
same book we find this passage:

In its true state (of unmodified, unshaped pri-
mordialness), Mind is naked, immaculate; not made of
anything, being of the Voidness; clear, vacuous, without
quality, transparent; timeless, uncompounded, unim-
peded, colorless (devoid of characteristic); not realizable as a separate thing, but as the unity of all things,
yet not composed of them; of one taste (i.e., of the Voidness, Thatness, or Ultimate Reality), and transcendent
over differentiation.

Evans-Wentz also comments here:

From the standpoint of Western science, particularly
of dynamics and physics, the ONE MIND is the unique
root of *energy* [capitals and italics mine] . . . the sole
dynamo of universal power, the initiator of vibrations . . .
the womb whence there come into being the cosmic rays
and matter in all its electronic aspects—as light, heat,
magnetism, electricity, radioactivity, or as organic and
inorganic substances in all their manifold guises, visible
and invisible, throughout the realm of nature.

Sir Arthur Eddington, in his "Nature of the Physical
World,"[31] has said:

110

In the scientific world the conception of substance is wholly lacking, and that which most nearly replaces it, viz., electric charge—is not exalted as star-performer above the other entities of physics. . . . To put the conclusion crudely—the stuff of the world is mind-stuff. . . . We may think of its nature as not altogether foreign to the feelings in our consciousness. Recognizing that the physical world is entirely abstract and without actuality apart from its linkage to consciousness, we restore consciousness to the fundamental position. This is not merely a philosophic doctrine but has become part of the scientific attitude of the day.

Govinda[11] says of Mind:

The dynamic forces of the Universe are not different from those of the human soul [mind], and to recognize and transform those forces in one's own mind—not only for one's own good, but for that of all living beings—is the aim of the Buddhist Tantras. . . . The starting point of Buddhist Yoga is neither cosmological nor of theologic-metaphysical character, but *psychological* in the deepest sense. (Italics mine.)

Milarepa has said:

> The mind is omnipotent like space;
> It illumines all manifestations as the
>   *Dharmakāya* [Body of Truth];
> It knows all and lightens all.
> I see it clearly like a crystal
> In my palm.[18]

Milarepa's insight sees the mind as transcending all such concepts as subjective, objective, extrovert, introvert, conscious or unconscious as formulated in modern psychology, although these concepts are well known to Buddhist thought.

Again Milarepa says:

> In the Mind-Essence, the quintessential "Light,"
> There is no adulteration by distracting thoughts.
> In the real nature of beings, the realm of Mind,
> There is no subject-object defilement.
> In the natural state of Mind-Essence
> There is no ground from which habitual
>   thought may rise.
>
> The nature of the mind is *Dharmakāya*!
> It is not defiled by forms
> And from attributes is free.

And from Mr. Chang's Commentary:[32]

> The main concern of Mahāmudrā, therefore, is the unfoldment of the true Essence of one's own mind.

This is not attempted, as in most meditation practices, by effortful mental concentration—where a single object or thought is held in the mind—but occurs spontaneously and naturally. Here the disciple may practice alone following his Guru's instructions, or be given a "pointing-out" demonstration to open his mind instantaneously, such as a push, a remark, a sudden exclamation, etc. Here we can see a striking resemblance to the practice and tradition of Zen, although there are certain differences in process and style.

Thus, through complete relaxation of mind and body—an utter "letting-go"—*awareness of Awareness itself* unfolds.

Those who are familiar with Zen teaching and methods will not find these ideas so very foreign or so very strange. *Detachment,* of course, is implicit in both teachings; and in Mahāmudrā, as in Zen, *Dhyāna* (the pure concentrative state achieved in meditation)—in its earlier stages often mistakenly overvalued by the beginner—is only preliminary to a realization of the goal. However pleasant or blissful it may be, ecstatic *Dhyāna* should never be *clung to,* as liable to plunge one into what is known as the "dead-void," where all awareness is lost. Milarepa speaks vividly of this matter in the following stanzas:[18]

> When your body is rightly posed, and your
>   mind absorbed in deep meditation,
> You may feel that thought and mind both
>   disappear;
> Yet this is but the surface experience of *Dhyāna.*
> By constant practice and mindfulness thereon,

113

One feels radiant Self-awareness shining like
    a brilliant lamp.
It is pure and bright as a flower,
It is like the feeling of staring
Into the vast and empty sky.
The Awareness of Voidness is limpid and
    transparent, yet vivid.
This Non-thought, this radiant and transparent
    experience
Is but the feeling of *Dhyāna*.
With this good foundation
One should further pray to [direct one's heart to]*
The Three Precious Ones [Buddha, Dharma,
    and Saṅgha],
And penetrate to Reality by deep thinking
    and contemplation [on *Śūnyatā,* or Voidness].
He thus can tie the Non-ego Wisdom
With the beneficial life-rope of deep *Dhyāna*.
With the power of kindness and compassion,
And with the altruistic vow of the Bodhi-heart,
He can see direct and clear
The truth of the enlightened Path
Of which nothing can be seen, yet all is
    clearly visioned.
He sees how wrong were the fears and hopes
    of his own mind.
Without arrival, he reaches the place of Buddha;
Without seeing, he visions the *Dharmakāya*;
Without effort, he does all things naturally.

* Prayers of supplication have no part in Buddhist practice,
but expressions of devotion, reverence, and gratitude for that
which we already are and have, do.

But in another of his Songs Milarepa also warns the beginner:

> Before you have realized Awareness in itself,
> Chatter not about the View of Voidness!
>
> All that which manifests
> Is unreal as an echo,
> Yet never fails to produce
> An effect that corresponds.
> Karmas and virtues, therefore,
> Should never be neglected.
>
> Before the great illumination
> Shines forth in your mind, cling not
> To sweet ecstasy and Voidness.
> Though all things are Void-manifesting,
> Never wallow in pleasures, nor expect
> Your troubles to vanish without effort.
>
> Things in themselves are void,
> So never cling to Voidness
> Lest you stray in formalism.
>
> When in the tide of mundane bliss
> One's crude, wandering thoughts subside,
> An ecstasy will then arise. But he
> Who is attached to it, will go astray.

In seeking to follow such teachings as these, a modern disciple, if at all possible, should train under a competent teacher or Guru; but if one cannot be found (as is so often the case in the West), the "Ten Suggestions" as given on pages 47-48 of *The*

Practice of Zen,[33] which are exceedingly helpful, and pertinent to the Kargyudpa teaching as well, will merit careful consideration by the serious student. If we are truly dedicated, the Buddha-Mind within will be our Teacher.

The "Ten Suggestions" are as follows:

⚘ Look inwardly at your state of mind before any thought arises.

⚘ When any thought does arise, cut it right off and bring your mind back to the work.

⚘ Try to look at the mind all the time.

⚘ Try to remember this "looking sensation" in daily activities.

⚘ Try to put your mind into a state as though you had just been shocked.

⚘ Meditate as frequently as possible.

⚘ Practice the "circle-running" exercise with your . . . friends.*

⚘ In the midst of the most tumultuous activities, stop and look at the mind for a moment.

⚘ Meditate for brief periods with the eyes wide open.

⚘ Read and reread as often as possible the *Prajñāpāramitā* Sūtras, such as the Diamond and Heart Sūtras, the *Prajñā* of Eight Thousand Verses, the *Mahāprajñāparamitā* Sūtra, etc.

* This exercise (see Chap. II of *The Practice of Zen,* Discourses of Master Hsu Yun), may be omitted if group practice is not feasible.

116

Dedicated practice on these ten suggestions should enable anyone to find out for himself what meditation, in the way of "serene reflection" as described by Hung Chih in the following poem,[34] really means. As *a clear Awareness in the tranquillity of No-thought,* as is Mahāmudrā also, it transcends all ordinary connotations.

Silently and serenely one forgets all words;
Clearly and vividly THAT appears before him.
When one realizes it, it is vast and without edges;
In its Essence, one is clearly aware.
Singularly reflecting is this bright awareness.
Full of wonder is this pure reflection.
Dew and the moon,
Stars and streams,
Snow on pine trees,
And clouds hovering on the mountain peaks—
From darkness, they all become glowingly bright;
From obscurity, they all turn to resplendent light.
Infinite wonder permeates this serenity;
In this Reflection all intentional efforts vanish.
Serenity is the final word [of all teachings];
Reflection is the response to all [manifestations].
Devoid of any effort,
This response is natural and spontaneous.
Disharmony will arise
If in reflection there is no serenity;
All will become wasteful and secondary
If in serenity there is no reflection.
The Truth of serene-reflection
Is perfect and complete.

Oh look! The hundred rivers flow
In tumbling torrents
To the great ocean!

For lack of space I have had to limit myself here
to a discussion, and to quotations from various
sources bearing directly, or indirectly, on Milarepa's
teachings and his relation thereto. I only wish there
were space to include extracts from the stories and
songs illustrative of the Master's humor; of his love
of the beautiful in the world of nature around him;
of his compassion, and tenderness toward all living
things. His contacts and contests with "demons" and
other "magic beings" were varied and numerous;
but we must remember that the ancient writings, in
common with *all* scriptures, are often couched in
esoteric or symbolic language—a kind of enigmatic
"code" familiar to all deep students and initiates,
and expressing everything from profound psychological experiences to the highest of spiritual and
metaphysical concepts in sometimes the most human
and earthy of terms. A prime example of this is the
greatly misunderstood and much criticized *Yab-
Yum,* or "Father-Mother" image, depicting a Bodhisattva and his consort in the bliss of conjugal
embrace. These figures do not represent human or
material entities, but *divine attributes* joined in the
Bliss of Cosmic Unity.* As Lobzang Jivaka[35] has

* For a comparable symbolism, see pp. 4-5, paragraph 3 under
"Fundamentals."

said: "The *Yab-Yum,* or *Dorje-Chang* . . . has nothing to do with sex or any fertility cult, but symbolizes
the union of Perfect Wisdom and Perfect Compassion, in other words, Enlightenment." He goes on
to say: "Similarly, the multitudinous representations
(of fierce, demon-like deities) are not grisly and
sadistic . . . but merely signify the vigorous conquest
of the lower self. Their reality rests not on external
facts or data but on the inner experiences of meditation." (See also reference to the *Ḍākinīs,* pp. 99-101.)

For true understanding one must sharpen one's
awareness of these facts. Milarepa knew this very
well and said, as has been reiterated again and again
in the *Bardo Thodol* (*The Tibetan Book of the
Dead*),[23] that *none* of these entities (gods, spirits,
demons, fairies, and the like) exist as concrete and
objective realities, but only *as symbols of deep
Cosmic truths* manifesting in the human mind and
emerging as thought-forms or projections from its
profoundest depths—in Jungian language, *arche-
types* arising from the hidden profundities of the
Unconscious. In the realm of the *Absolute,* the
Dharmadhātu, nothing—as we are capable of knowing or imagining it on this relative plane—exists.
As Milarepa has said, *in the light of Ultimate Reality,*
our lives right here and now are as illusory and
dream-like as an echo!

By the same token, according to this understanding, "spirits" of the "dead" (the "Hungry
Ghosts," or "Restless Spirits" of the Tibetan "Wheel

of Life") or other visions as manifested through the Unconscious to our minds and senses, although they may not always be purely subjective, have only a relative and transient existence. Obviously, in this view, there is no "death" in the sense of annihilation; only growth and change—*evolution* if you will. Even science says as much. Realizing this, the problem of personal "survival" on that semi-earthbound plane which is called by some the "Astral," loses much of its importance, although it need not be denied or ignored if one sees it for what it is, and does not get "bogged down" in it. This is a danger the Masters are forever warning us against. They are aiming *beyond* this, for that transcendent, inexpressible Reality—of another dimension altogether—for which our brains have no concepts, and of which the vision, at best, is but a symbolic representation. Compared to *this*, concrete "appearances" (visionary or otherwise), lose much of their value. Whether they are "real" or not depends upon how one looks at them!

In speaking of the life and teaching of Milarepa, I have tried to convey, as best I could, some small impression of the spirit and stature of this great Buddhist, who arose at a time and in a setting very strange to us, yet whose breadth of vision, prophetic insight, and love of Truth cross every barrier of time, space, and cultural tradition.

Knowing that mankind had already entered the age of decline—the *Kali-Yuga,* or "dark-age" in which the Spirit is veiled deeply under the flesh— Milarepa reiterated the following prophetic words, spoken to him long before by his Guru, Marpa—all this, remember, in a remote part of Asia nearly a thousand years ago:

> He said: "At the time of defilement,
> When declines the Buddha's teaching,
> Lives will be short and merits poor.
> Evils and hindrances, in myriad forms,
> Will o'ershadow all the world;
> Leisure and long life will become most rare;
> Knowledge will [expand] to a point
> Too stupendous to comprehend;
> Proofs and conclusions will be hard to reach.
> To understand the truth of Tantra will be
>   most difficult.
> Therefore, my son, try nothing else,
> But work hard at the practice!"[18]

How true all this is of our world today! Here, if nowhere else, is food for thought.

While Milarepa taught and practiced the Vajrayāna form of Buddhism, both the Path of Means (*the Six Yogas of Nāropā*) and the Path of Liberation (*Mahāmudrā*) (which converge in the higher stages), this was not all. He never forgot the *foundations* upon which *all* Schools of Buddhism rest (see Chapter I): reverence for Gautama the

Buddha, recitation and understanding of the Three Refuges (actually *four* in the Tibetan form—for here refuge in the Guru is added) (see pp. 32-33), the Four Noble Truths, the Eight-fold Path, the Twelve-fold Chain of Dependent Origination, the Precepts and Pāramitās, the emptiness of Ego—and above all, the essential unity of Wisdom and Compassion. Of course the *Bodhisattva Vow,* dedication to the salvation of all beings, was stressed in the living of the perfect Buddhist "Way of Life." In fact there was no level or type of human understanding for which Milarepa did not have a pertinent and helpful teaching—a means for guidance and progress on the Path. His was *a synthesis of the essentials in all Buddhist Schools.* But above everything he counseled PRACTICE (the Kargyudpa is also known as "The Practice Succession"), for without the practice of *what we know,* he tells us, however little that may be—without the destruction of *ego-clinging* and the seeds of "habitual-thinking" in the *Ālaya,* or Store-Consciousness, without the cultivation of our deeper intuitive faculties and spiritual awareness, without the active use of understanding and compassion toward *all* our fellow beings, animal as well as human—intellectual knowledge *alone* will avail us little on the Path of Bodhi, and liberation from the Wheel of Birth-and-Death becomes impossible. This does not mean that thought and study should be neglected—far from it; reflection and knowledge are very necessary parts of our foundation—but only

122

that the *primary emphasis,* after one has passed the stage of initial inquiry, should be placed upon INSIGHT and ENLIGHTENMENT (*Bodhi-citta*—the Wisdom-Heart, the Enlightened Consciousness) gained through some form of daily practice and meditation —wherever or on whatever level we find ourselves *today.* The benefits derived therefrom will make themselves felt in a wonderful way, and lead to greater ones—even in the busiest of everyday human lives.

Milarepa spoke of the necessity of self-discipline, of a humble and loving heart, of awareness of the transiency and emptiness of all compounded things, of the Ultimate Reality of the Buddhahood within us and the possibility of its realization in this very life, and of the Illuminating Void of MIND itself —the origin and matrix of all manifested things— where giver and receiver, subject and object, high and low, this and that, meditation and meditator— all dichotomies and dualities—interfuse, and are dissolved in transcendent Light. Buddhahood is not *attained,* but UNFOLDED—if need be step by step— starting *now* with the means we have at hand and growing through practice to the point where all "means" may be discarded, even as is the raft when we have crossed to the Other Shore, and beyond. This is the "gradual Path" he pointed out to those whose natures require it.

But the *ultimate* way, by-passing all "means," exertive efforts, and even "stages," is MAHĀMUDRĀ—

Direct Awareness of the Essence of Mind itself. This is the highest pinnacle of the Kargyudpa teachings.

The "Songs'" translator comments: "Milarepa's life is an unmistakable testimony to the unity and interdependence of *all* the essential teachings of Buddhism—Theravāda, Mahāyāna, and Vajrayāna. Among his many great contributions, this is unique, and perhaps the greatest of them all."[18]

In conclusion I would like to quote four brief stanzas from the "Songs"[18]—one from a song of Milarepa, the other three sung by his disciple, Rachungpa; and finally, Milarepa's "Song of Departure" to his patrons, the villagers of Nya Non.

Milarepa's stanza:

> To give alms to the needy with compassion
> Is equal to serving Buddhas in the Three Times.*
> To give with sympathy to beggars is
> To make offerings to Milarepa.
> Sentient beings are one's parents; to
> Discriminate between them is harmful and
> Ignorant. True sages and
> Scholars are always in accord;
> Clinging to one's own School and condemning
>   others
> Is the certain way to waste one's learning.
> Since all Dharmas are equally good,
> Those who cling to sectarianism
> Degrade Buddhism and sever

* Past, present, and future.

124

Themselves from Liberation.
All the happiness one has
Is derived from others;
All the help one gives to them
In return brings happiness.
One's pernicious deeds
Only harm oneself.

Rachungpa's stanzas:

The rivers of India and Nepal,
Divided by different valleys,
Flow in different directions.
Yet, as rivers, they are all alike—
In the great ocean they will meet again.

Divided by the Four Continents,
The sun rises in the East, the moon
Sets in the West; as light-bearers
They are both alike—on a cloudless
Autumn evening they sometimes see each other.

Veiled by ignorance,
The minds of man and Buddha
Appear to be different.
Yet in the realm of Mind-Essence
They are both of one taste. Some-
Time they will meet each other
In the great *Dharmadhātu*.

Milarepa's Song of Departure:

In the immense blue sky above
Roll on the sun and moon. Their

Courses mark the change of time.
Blue sky, I wish you health and fortune,
For I, the moon-and-sun, am leaving
To visit the Four Continents for pleasure.

On the mountain peak is a great rock
Round which oft the vulture circles,
The king of birds. Their meeting
And their parting mark the change of time.
Dear rock, be well and healthy, for I,
The vulture, now will fly away
Into the vast space for pleasure.
May lightnings never strike you,
May I not be caught by snares.
Inspired by the Dharma,
May we soon meet again
In prosperity and boon.

Below in the Tsang River
Swim fish with golden eyes;
Their meeting and their parting
Mark the change of time.
Dear stream, be well and healthy, for I, the fish
Am leaving for the Ganges for diversion.
May irrigators never drain you,
May fishermen n'er net me.
Inspired by the Dharma,
May we soon meet again
In prosperity and boon.

In the fair garden blooms the flower, Halo;
Circling round it is the Persian bee.
Their meeting and their parting
Mark the change of time.

Dear flower, be well and healthy, for I
Will see the Ganges' blooms for pleasure.
May hail not beat down upon you,
May winds blow me not away.
Inspired by the Dharma,
May we soon meet again
In prosperity and boon.

Circling round the Yogi Milarepa
Are the faithful patrons from Nya Non.
Their meeting and their parting
Mark the change of time.
Be well and healthy, dear patrons, as I
Leave for the mountains for diversion.
May I, the Yogi, make good progress,
May you, my patrons, live long.
Inspired by the Dharma,
May we soon meet again
In prosperity and boon!

4

IN RETROSPECT:
A DHARMA JOURNEY[36]

In looking back along the road that led to my becoming a Buddhist, and later a Tibetan Buddhist of the Kargyudpa School, my first thought was: "How singularly quiet, gradual, and undramatic most of my experiences were!" But perhaps in this very fact may lie something (if I can only find it!) of value to others whose climb has been as long, at times imperceptible, and often as stumbling as mine.

I remember events and experiences in the past (of a type not unique to me, of course) which seemed at the time to be entirely negative but which, in retrospect, I now realize served a deeply constructive purpose. Like many other "seekers in the dark," my self-directed steps often wandered into strange by-ways. But I learned lessons thereby.

I can see now that each experience, even the "negative" ones, was part of a building process, going on often in spite of myself and of any errors I might make along the way. It was as though I had been guided, without conscious awareness, along a path known to a higher Consciousness—at one level part of myself (the Buddha-Mind within), at another, transcending "myself" and all that could be knowable to me. It was as if this Presence, permeating everything yet in itself no-thing, were always there. At length I came to a realization of the significance of this paradox: If I listened, I was guided; but the *steps* had to be my own. If I failed to listen, I went astray; but even then, a Power beyond myself yet always within myself never failed to bring me back, although the time (as we reckon human time) may have been long.

I remember a strange experience I had years ago, before I understood or knew anything of Buddhism except for the vaguest conceptions (some quite erroneous) gained from a novel or a travel book or two. I had no knowledge of Sanskrit names nor of Buddhist philosophy; but I was drawn to the East. In this experience, the Mahābodhisattva Avalokiteśvara (the Patron Buddha of Tibet), of whom I had never heard, spoke to me mentally

129

(though inaudibly in any physical sense) through the agency of an inspired picture, giving me his name. I got it recognizably though imperfectly as "Avalokit(a)." Later I found that Avalokiteśvara (or Avalokita, his shortened name) means "one who is gazed at," or "one who gazes (with compassion)"—exactly what had been happening here. I "felt" the words: *I have been with you since the day you were born*; I saw nothing but the picture; but I understood. As an aspect of the Buddha-Mind, the personification of Wisdom and Compassion in One Essence, Avalokiteśvara was immanent within and at the same time transcendent without—a Presence to which I could always turn. My earlier intuitions had become manifest.

Later I realized that this must have been an experience of deep significance—little as I understood it then—a manifestation of the *Sambhogakāya* (the spiritual "Body of Bliss" of the Bodhisattva, and "Vehicle of Divine Power"—the second of the "Three Bodies of Buddha"),* clairaudiently received.

In time, as an extension of this experience and through the help of my teacher—to whom I owe an inestimable debt of gratitude (although I, alone, am responsible for whatever may be written here)—I

* See p. 55.

found my Patron Bodhisattva, Tārā ("Dölma the Merciful"), Tibet's Protectress and "Goddess of Mercy," who, as I have quoted before, "extends her loving care to the good and the bad, the wise and the foolish, like the sun that shines for sinners as well as for saints"[11]* She, as an emanation of Avalokiteśvara, is at-one with him and so, in Essence, at-one with me and with all beings. This process of Identification, as I have mentioned earlier in this book, is one of the many means by which, in Tibetan meditation, the disciple may realize the Buddha-nature within himself and within all sentient life.

I also truly feel that every disciple, when he is ready, will one day find the *Nirmanakāya* too—the visible, manifested "Body of Buddha" (as Śākyamuni himself was), in the person of an earthly Guru.

By this Path—through reverence for the *Nirmanakāya* and identification in meditation with the *Sambhogakāya*—the disciple is led to a realization of his Oneness-in-Essence with the *Dharmakāya*, the "Body-of-the-Law"—the One Absolute Reality—of which the noumenal (*Sambhogakāya*) and the phenomenal (*Nirmanakāya*) are aspects. "Your, yourself, are Buddha" is no idle bit of philosophy. Through Form we reach the Formless, through "Body,

* See also pp. 100-101.

Speech, and Mind" we reach "No-mind"—that Other Shore, and beyond, where all "rafts" may be left behind. Few, certainly not myself, can attain the Unborn at one bound; most of us must grow, through living practice, toward the realization of Ultimate Truth.

Thus the Tibetan Yogic method, based for a thousand years upon the use and development of man's finest psychophysical energies, has proved its value, for me, and for others like me, at every stage on the Bodhi-Path. It leads to, and may—for those who are ready and prepared—be combined with or even superseded by that ultimate form of medita-tion—"spontaneous, effortless, and natural"—known in the Kargyudpa School as *Mahāmudrā*, the Great Symbol, "in which no object whatsover is held in the meditator's mind, and no thought save the awareness of Mind itself."[18]

Milarepa, Tibet's great Poet-Saint, has said:

Buddha [the Essence of Buddhahood] cannot be
    found by searching,
    So contemplate your own MIND.[18]*

And Mr. Chang, in his Commentary in the same book, adds:

* See also p. 109.

"The main concern of Mahāmudrā, therefore, is the unfoldment of the true Essence of one's own mind."

Here "all subject-object dualities are transcended in pure Awareness"[18]—the awarenes of Awareness itself. This is the ultimate Path, in which the "Three Bodies of Buddha" are seen as *One*—and in the end, even that One is transcended.

Comparable experiences are found, of course, in other Buddhist disciplines, regardless of School or sect—the true Essence of the Buddha-Dharma is the same for all. But as I implied at the beginning, it may be helpful to those who find the way long, who feel they are "getting nowhere," to realize that to "get somewhere"' is beside the point. As long as we are on the Bodhi-Path, no matter how long the way may seem and no matter how small our understanding may appear at any given moment, there is no need to struggle to "get somewhere." *We are already There.* We need only to "let go"—to live our lives in word, thought, and deed at the highest level we are capable of *now*, and to be what in reality we already *are*. The rest will come without struggle, when our readiness to receive it grows. By knowing in heart and mind that we are Buddha now, that

we live and share in the Essence of everything that
is and, most importantly, by *practicing* this knowledge in daily life and in *meditation,* we have already
entered the "Gateless Gate" and found the Path
which leads to Ultimate Enlightenment.

This is the ineffable vista, attainable to all, that
my own small Dharma journey has revealed to me.

FROM THE WELL OF MEDITATION[37]

Dead names and personal attributes
Belong neither to Action nor to Reality;
The perfect name is No-name,
And the perfect action is without motive.

Be relaxed in deep things
And quiet in little things,
Like a pond whose shallow water
Pictures the still bottom as a glass admits light,
And whose deep water
Moves not with the ruffling wind.
Have no thought, but let the answer
Rise to the surface
As bubbles rise
From the lake-bottom springs.

The awakened mind
Neither thinks nor speculates—
The awakened mind
Knows.

Silver and gold are kindred metals,
But who can strike a light from them?
The answer is given in an instant—
Without thought.

Understand without effort
And move without struggle;
Thus does the mind manifest itself
And no thing is there to be manifested.

The awakened mind
Neither thinks nor speculates—
Void is it,
And without form;
Void it is,
And no attribute is there.

The wind blows,
But no hand catches it;
The thunder rolls,
But whither goes the sound?

Pride and ego mask the inner light,
And no cloud of earth can equal them;
Rain falls from these clouds,
And the hours know but tears.

Who is it that weeps
And cannot move the barrier?
Find that one—if you can!
Heaven and Hell are not his hiding place,
Nor does the earth harbor him;
Only the shadows cover him,
And nothing is there.

The ball is tossed,
And the player catches it;
But no hand catches
The answer to vain desires.

Under the mantle of *Māyā* (illusion)
Who can see the stars?
Under the ego-shadow
Who can find the light?
Silver and gold are kindred metals,
But who can strike a light from them?

Regard a woven garment—
Never can it clothe the mind.
Regard a valued trinket—
Never can it pay for wasted days.

The hand holds a key,
But the fingers close upon it
And it vanishes;
The mind holds an answer,
But thought grasps it
And there is nothing there.

Pay the price of silence
And a thousand voices answer;
Speak,
And silence alone replies.

Great Space without
At first seems to be Voidness;
But Voidness is within—
And only the mind can compass it.

This song is no-song—
Why seek for a meaning?
The questions were answered
Before ever a word was spoken.

KEY
TO TRANSLITERATION OF
SANSKRIT TERMS

All terms in the text have been rendered into the standard system of transliteration, a key to which is given below:

Vowels

a   as vowel sound in "but".

ā   as in "father".

i   as in "kin".

ī   as vowel sound in "seen".

u   as in "put".

ū   as vowel sound in "hoot".

ṛi   is the slightly trilled sound of "ri" found more heavily trilled in Spanish and Italian.

e   as vowel sound in "make".

ai   as vowel sound in "kite".

o   as in "boat".

au   as the combined sound o and u.

Consonants (only relevant ones are given).

ṃ   nasalized sound between "m" and "ng". Pronounce "sung" without closing the throat.

c   as "ch" in child.

ñ   pronounced with tongue on roof of mouth directly behind upper teeth. No exact English equivalent.

ḍ, ṭ, and ṇ   pronounced as d, t, and n with tongue turned upward and backward along the palate. No exact English equivalents.

ś   as "sh" in "shirt".

ṣ   pronounced as "sh" but with tongue turned upward and backward as for ḍ, ṭ, and ṇ.

jñ   as "gu" in "guest".

Aspirates, such as "dh" and "bh" are pronounced with a slight exhalation of air as in adhesion and abhor. All other consonants are pronounced as in English.

NOTES

1 The second paragraph of this Foreword, "Why I Became a Buddhist," first appeared in the May, 1970, issue of *The Middle Way*, London, in reply to the many questions I have been asked about Buddhism and my own dedication, as a Westerner, to the Buddha's philosophy and Way of Life.

2 An earlier version of this Chapter appeared as an article under the title, "Buddhism for the West," in *The Maha Bodhi Journal*, Calcutta, May-June, 1966.

3 For a fuller exposition of this subject, see "The Central Conception of Buddhism and the Meaning of the Word 'Dharma,'" by Th. Stcherbatsky, Royal Asiatic Society, London; or *Buddhism*, Richard A. Gard, Ed., Prentice-Hall International, London, 1961, and George Braziller, Inc., New York, 1961, pp. 110-112.

4 Nyanaponika Thera, *The Heart of Buddhist Meditation, Based on the Buddha's Way of Mindfulness*, Rider & Co., London, 1969.

5 Rear Admiral E. H. Shattock, *An Experiment in Mindfulness—An English Admiral's Experiences in a Buddhist Monastery*, E. P. Dutton & Co., Inc., New York, 1960.

6 Christmas Humphreys, *A Popular Dictionary of Buddhism*, The Citadel Press, New York, 1963.

7 *Saṃyutta-nikāya*, Vol. ii, p. 19.

8   Based on an article by the author that appeared in *The World Buddhism Vesak Annual,* Ceylon, 1969.

9   Ananda Commaraswamy, *Buddha and the Gospel of Buddhism,* University Books, Long Island, N.Y., 1964.

10 Christmas Humphreys, *Buddhism,* Penguin Books Ltd., a Pelican Original, London, 1957.

11 Lama Anagarika Govinda, *Foundations of Tibetan Mysticism,* Rider & Co., London, 1959.

12 I have no space to go into further detail here, but enlightening accounts may be found in the literature, notably in Govinda's *Foundation of Tibetan Mysticism* and Blofeld's *The Wheel of Life* (Rider & Co., London, 1959).

13 Based upon an article by the author which appeared in *The Mountain Path,* Tiruvannamalai, Madras, April, 1967.

14 Dr. D. T. Suzuki, "The Development of Mahāyāna Buddhism," Part II, *The Middle Way,* London, November, 1966.

15 Based on an article that appeared in *The Mountain Path,* Tiruvannamalai, Madras, July, 1966, and later was reprinted in *The Maha Bodhi Journal,* Calcutta, November, 1968.

16 This Chapter is based on a lecture given before the Friends of Buddhism, Washington, D.C., in 1964 and on three shorter articles published, respectively, by *The Maha Bodhi Journal,* Calcutta, in 1967, and *The Mountain Path,* Madras, in 1967 and 1968.

17 For a detailed account, derived from original sources, of Milarepa's life, teachings, ministry, and the times and milieu in which he lived, see W. Y. Evans-Wentz, *Tibet's Great Yogi, Milarepa,* Oxford University Press, London, 1958.

18 *The Hundred Thousand Songs of Milarepa,* in 2 volumes, translated from the original Tibetan, and annotated, with commentary by Garma C. C. Chang, University Books, Long Island, N.Y., 1962.

19 The story of Gambopa and his teachings may be found in Herbert V. Guenther's *The Jewel Ornament of Liberation,* Rider & Co., London, 1959.

20 See Note 18, Vol. II, p. 679.

21 See Note 18. The other short quotations in this section are also taken from Mr. Chang's book.

22 See W. Y. Evans-Wentz, *The Tibetan Book of the Dead,* facing pages 118 and 136 with text references indicated; Charles Poncé's *The Nature of the I Ching* (Award Books, N.Y., and Tandem Books, London, 1970, pp. 82-83); Guiseppe Tucci's *The Theory and Practice of the Maṇḍala,* Rider & Co., London, 1966; and Lama Anagarika Govinda's *Foundations of Tibetan Mysticism* throughout.

23 W. Y. Evans-Wentz, *Tibetan Series: The Tibetan Book of the Great Liberation* (1954); *The Tibetan Book of the Dead* (3rd Edition, 1957); *Tibetan Yoga and Secret Doctrines* (2nd Edition, 1958) including Chang's "Yogic Commentary" therein; and *Tibet's Great Yogi, Milarepa* (2nd Edition, 1958). Oxford University Press, London.

24 Garma C. C. Chang, *Teachings of Tibetan Yoga,* University Books, Long Island, N.Y., 1962.

25 Edward Conze, *Buddhist Meditation,* George Allen & Unwin Ltd., London, 1956.

26 Mircea Eliade, *Yoga: Immortality and Freedom,* Bollingen Series LVI, Pantheon Books, New York, 1958.

27 Edward Conze, *Buddhism—Its Essence and Devel-*

opment, Bruno Cassirer, Oxford, 1953; Harper, New York, 1959.

28 See Note 18, Appendix, Vol. II, p. 683 ff.

29 See Note 18, Appendix.

30 Chang Chen-chi, *The Practice of Zen*, Harper Brothers, New York, 1959.

31 Sir Arthur Eddington, *Nature of the Physical World*, Cambridge University Press, American Branch, New York, 1947.

32 See Note 18, Appendix, Vol. II, p. 683 ff., and Notes referring to Mahāmudrā, throughout the book.

33 Chang Chen-chi, *The Practice of Zen*, Harper Brothers, New York, 1959; Rider & Co., London, 1960. The "Suggestions" will be found on p. 59 of the British edition.

34 From *Notes on Serene Reflection*, by the famous Zen Master, Hung Chih, of the Tsao Tung (Jap.: Soto) School. See reference 33, p. 46 (p. 57 in the British edition).

35 Quoted in *The Middle Way*, London, February, 1964, courtesy *France-Asie*, Tokyo.

36 This essay, in part, was published in *The Middle Way*, London, November, 1967.

37 This poem, in the Zen spirit as I feel it, was first published in *The Golden Light*, Penang, and later reprinted in *The Mountain Path*, Tiruvannamalai, Madras.

38 See a most significant new contribution to this study: Garma C. C. Chang's *The Buddhist Teaching of Totality—The Philosophy of Hwa Yen Buddhism*, Pennsylvania State University Press, University Park, Pa., and London, 1971.

BIBLIOGRAPHY

Ashvaghosha, *The Awakening of Faith,* trans. by Timothy Richard, Alan Hull Walton, Ed., Foreword by Aldous Huxley, Chas. Skilton, London, 1961.

Benoit, Hubert, *The Supreme Doctrine—Psychological Studies in Zen Thought,* Foreword by Aldous Huxley, The Viking Press, New York, 1959.

Blofeld, John R. (Tr.), *I Ching, The Book of Change,* Geo. Allen & Unwin, London, 1965.

Blofeld, John R., *The Tantric Mysticism of Tibet,* E. P. Dutton & Co., New York, 1970.

————— *The Wheel of Life,* Rider & Co., London, 1959.

————— *The Zen Teaching of Huang Po,* Grove Press, New York, 1959.

Chang Chen-chi, *The Practice of Zen,* Harper & Brothers, New York, 1959; Rider & Co., London, 1960.

Chang, Garma C. C., *The Buddhist Teaching of Totality —The Philosophy of Hwa Yen Buddhism,* Pennsylvania State University Press, University Park, Pa., and London, 1971

————— *The Hundred Thousand Songs of Milarepa,* trans. from the original Tibetan, with Commentary and Notes by the author. University Books, Long Island, N.Y., 1962.

————— *Teachings of Tibetan Yoga,* University Books, Long Island, N.Y., 1962.

Conze, Edward, *Buddhism, Its Essence and Develop-*

ment, Bruno Cassirer, Ltd., Oxford, 1953; Harper Torchbooks, New York, 1959.

————— *Buddhist Meditation,* Geo. Allen & Unwin, London, 1956.

————— *A Short History of Buddhism,* Chetana, Bombay, India, 1960.

Coomaraswamy, Ananda, *Buddha and the Gospel of Buddhism,* University Books, Long Island, N.Y., 1964.

David-Neel, Alexandra, *Secret Oral Teaching of Tibetan Buddhist Sects,* The Maha Bodhi Society, Calcutta, India, 1964.

————— *Magic and Mystery in Tibet,* University Books, Long Island, N.Y., 1958.

————— *Initiations and Initiates in Tibet,* University Books, Long Island, N.Y., 1959.

Eddington, Sir Arthur, *The Nature of the Physical World,* Cambridge University Press, American Branch, New York, 1942.

Eliade, Mircea, *Yoga, Immortality, and Freedom,* Bollingen Series LVI, Pantheon Books, New York, 1958.

Evans-Wentz, W. Y., *Tibetan Series: The Tibetan Book of the Dead,* 3rd ed., with Commentaries by C. G. Jung, Anagarika Govinda, and Sir John Woodruffe, 1957; *The Tibetan Book of the Great Liberation,* with Psychological Commentary by C. G. Jung, 1954; *Tibet's Great Yogi, Milarepa,* 2nd ed., 1958; *Tibetan Yoga and Secret Doctrines,* 2nd ed., with Foreword by R. R. Marett and Yogic Commentary by Chang Chen-chi, 1958; Oxford University Press, London.

Gard, Richard A., *Buddhism,* George Braziller, Inc., New York, 1961; Prentice-Hall International, Inc., London, 1961.

Goddard, Dwight, *A Buddhist Bible* (translations from

the Sūtras), E. P. Dutton & Co., Inc., New York, 1952.

Govinda, Anagarika, *Foundations of Tibetan Mysticism,* Rider & Co., London, 1959.

———— *The Way of the White Clouds—A Buddhist Pilgrim in Tibet,* Hutchinson of London, 1966.

Guenther, H. V., *The Jewel Ornament of Liberation* (Gambopa's teachings), Rider & Co., London, 1959.

Herrigel, Eugene, *The Method of Zen,* Pantheon Books, New York, 1960.

Humphreys, Christmas, *Buddhism,* a Pelican Original, 3rd ed., Penguin Books, Ltd., London, 1962.

———— *A Popular Dictionary of Buddhism,* The Citadel Press, New York, 1963.

———— *The Sūtra of Wei Lang (Hui Neng),* trans. by Wong Mou-Lam, Revised Edition, Luzac & Co., London, 1953.

————. Ed., *The Wisdom of Buddhism—An Anthology,* Random House, New York, 1961.

Jivaka, Lobzang, *Imji Getsul—An English Buddhist in a Tibetan Monastery,* Routledge & Kegan Paul, London, 1962.

Luk, Charles (Lu K'uan Yü), *Ch'an and Zen Teaching,* (a *Series* in 3 volumes, 1960, 1961, and 1962), Rider & Co., London.

———— *The Secrets of Chinese Meditation,* Rider & Co., London, 1964.

Maraini, Fosco, *Secret Tibet,* Grove Press, New York, 1960.

Masunaga, Reiho, *The Soto Approach to Zen,* Layman Buddhist Soc. Press, Tokyo, 1958.

Nyanaponika Thera, *The Heart of Buddhist Meditation,* Rider & Co., London, 1969.

Pallis, Marco, *Peaks and Lamas,* Knopf, New York, 1949.

Piyadassi Thera, *The Buddha's Ancient Path*, Rider & Co., London, 1964.

Poncé, Charles, *The Nature of the I Ching*, Award Books, N.Y., and Tandem Books, London, 1970.

Rahula, Walpola, *What the Buddha Taught*, Gordon Fraser, London, 1959.

Ross, Nancy Wilson, *Three Ways of Asian Wisdom*, Simon & Shuster, New York, 1966.

Sharma, Chandradhar, *Indian Philosophy—A Critical Survey*, Barnes & Noble, New York, 1962.

Shattock, E. H., *An Experiment in Mindfulness* (an English Admiral's experience in a [Burmese] Buddhist Monastery), E. P. Dutton & Co., Inc., New York, 1960.

Snellgrove, David, *Buddhist Himālaya—Travels and Studies in Quest of the Origins and Nature of Tibetan Religion*, Philosophical Library, New York, 1957.

Suzuki, Beatrice Lane, *Mahāyāna Buddhism: A Brief Outline* (with an Introduction by Daisetz Teitaro Suzuki, and a Foreword by Christmas Humphreys), The Macmillan Co., New York, 1959.

Suzuki, D. T., *The Essence of Buddhism*, The Buddhist Society, London, 1957.

———— *Studies in the Lankavatara Sūtra*, Routledge & Kegan Paul Ltd., London, 1957.

———— *The Training of a Zen Buddhist Monk*, University Books, New York, 1959.

———— *Outlines of Mahāyāna Buddhism*, Schocken Books, New York, 1963.

Trungpa, Chögyam, *Born in Tibet*, Geo. Allen & Unwin, London, 1966.

Tucci, Guiseppe, *The Theory and Practice of the Maṇḍala* (trans. from the Italian by Alan H. Broderick), Rider & Co., London, 1961.